Classic Toys
in Wood

Projects & Plans

Janet & Richard Strombeck

 Sterling Publishing Co., Inc. New York

This book is dedicated to our children, whose help and judgments were invaluable, to their children, who were pure inspiration, and to children of all ages everywhere.

Drafting by Joe Heller

Library of Congress Cataloging-in-Publication Data

Strombeck, Janet.
    Classic toys in wood : projects & plans. / by Janet A. Strombeck & Richard H. Strombeck.
        p.   cm.
    "Portions of this work originally appeared in The Ström toys published in 1983 by Sterling Publishing"—T.p. verso.
    Includes index.
    ISBN 0-8069-0622-7
    1. Wooden toy making.   I. Strombeck, Richard.   II. Strombeck, Janet.   Ström toys.   III. Title.
    TT174.5.W6S768   1994
    745.592—dc20
                                                        94–25808
                                                        CIP

10   9   8   7   6   5   4   3   2   1

Published by Sterling Publishing Company, Inc.
387 Park Avenue South, New York, N.Y. 10016
Portions of this work originally appeared in
The Ström Toys published in 1983 by Sterling Publishing
© 1994 by Sun Designs/Rexstrom, Inc.
Distributed in Canada by Sterling Publishing
% Canadian Manda Group, One Atlantic Avenue, Suite 105
Toronto, Ontario, Canada M6K 3E7
Distributed in Great Britain by Cassell PLC
Villiers House, 41/47 Strand, London WC2N 5JE, England
Distributed in Australia by Capricorn Link (Australia) Pty Ltd.
P.O. Box 6651, Baulkham Hills, Business Centre, NSW 2153, Australia
Manufactured in the United States of America

Sterling ISBN 0-8069-0622-7

Contents

FOREWORD

Following our tradition of publishing designs and plans for things that are unusual and hard to find, we have put together this extraordinary collection of wooden toys. I'm sure many of you already know our affection for wood and the many fine products and pleasures that come from it. Wooden toys are no exception.

In an earlier time, well-designed wooden toys were built by a father or grandfather and traditionally passed down to succeeding generations. These having survived, are now cherished family heirlooms. Broken parts were repaired or replaced and the toys lasted through years of play and use.

Today's high impact, injection molded toys are also long-lived even though programmed for early obsolescence. But, once they begin to crack, split, melt or warp, they are for all practical purposes irrecoverable.

It has been our opinion that many people prefer wooden toys for their children, and in fact would take the time to build them if the toy design and function were to their liking. Interest in wooden toy construction by home craftsmen is growing. Witness to this fact is the large number of wooden toy books now on the market. Most of these books supply instruction for relatively quick toy projects, taking three to four hours maximum.

We believe the toy designs in this book are different from what is available elsewhere. All have been designed and built in our home workshop; all are of *simple* construction. They do require more than three or four hours. *Not* because they are more complicated, but because they have more detail and finishing.

Many of the toys in this book can be completed with only hand tools. We used both hand and power tools. The principal power tools we used are a radial arm saw, sabre saw, jig saw, small belt sander and a small drill press. A small inexpensive wood lathe was used to make the wooden wagon wheels. I encourage *all of you*, young and old, men and women, to try a toy project. *Everyone* can do it, and you already have plans right here to start with.

Most of the toys are made from fir, and a good number of them just from fir scraps, but hardwood can be used and is recommended for some toys such as the wagon.

Even though we live on a lake and have a sand beach in our front yard, we know that weather and supervision requirements of young children limit their time outside, especially by water. Consequently, we have intended most of these toys to be what I call "rug" toys. When they are being "worked" indoors, large navy beans, for example, can be used in place of sand.

Complete construction plans are available for *all* wooden toys shown. If a toy has a part or parts that we feel are not readily available at a local source, we have included these parts with the plan package. Other parts are available from your local stores. If you cannot make a particular part, call us. The SUN DESIGNS number is 414-567-4255.

Good luck with your projects, and we'd be delighted to see a picture of your finished product. We sincerely hope that your children or grandchildren will have as much enjoyment from your efforts as ours have had.

CLASSIC TOYS IN WOOD

BANK
Simple but intriguing.
See if the kids can solve the mystery of the disappearing coins! Size 5″ high, 4″ wide.

BANK

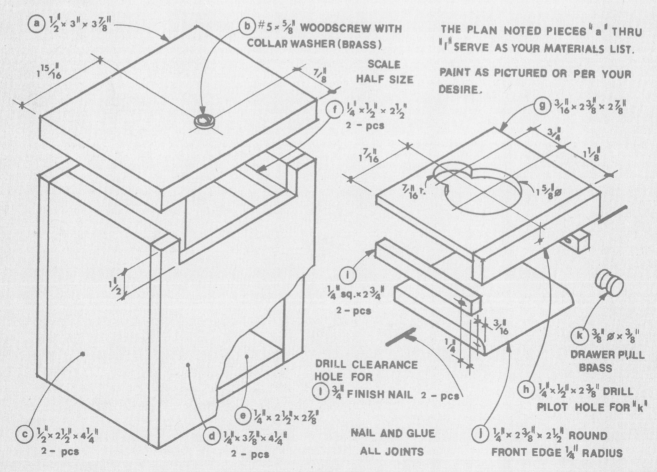

(a) $\frac{1}{2}'' \times 3'' \times 3\frac{7}{8}''$

(b) #5 × $\frac{5}{8}''$ WOODSCREW WITH COLLAR WASHER (BRASS)

SCALE HALF SIZE

$1\frac{15}{16}''$

$\frac{7}{8}''$

(f) $\frac{1}{4}'' \times \frac{1}{2}'' \times 2\frac{1}{2}''$ 2 - pcs

THE PLAN NOTED PIECES "a" THRU "l" SERVE AS YOUR MATERIALS LIST.

PAINT AS PICTURED OR PER YOUR DESIRE.

(g) $\frac{3}{16}'' \times 2\frac{3}{8}'' \times 2\frac{7}{8}''$

$\frac{3}{4}''$

$1\frac{1}{8}''$

$1\frac{7}{16}''$

$\frac{7}{16}''$

$1\frac{5}{8}'' \varnothing$

$1\frac{1}{2}''$

(l) $\frac{1}{4}''$ sq. × $2\frac{3}{4}''$ 2 - pcs

$\frac{3}{16}''$

$\frac{1}{4}''$

(k) $\frac{3}{8}'' \varnothing \times \frac{3}{8}''$ DRAWER PULL BRASS

DRILL CLEARANCE HOLE FOR (l) $\frac{3}{4}''$ FINISH NAIL 2 - pcs

(h) $\frac{1}{4}'' \times \frac{1}{2}'' \times 2\frac{3}{8}''$ DRILL PILOT HOLE FOR "k"

(c) $\frac{1}{2}'' \times 2\frac{1}{2}'' \times 4\frac{1}{4}''$ 2 - pcs

(e) $\frac{1}{4}'' \times 2\frac{1}{2}'' \times 2\frac{7}{8}''$

(d) $\frac{1}{4}'' \times 3\frac{7}{8}'' \times 4\frac{1}{4}''$ 2 - pcs

NAIL AND GLUE ALL JOINTS

(j) $\frac{1}{4}'' \times 2\frac{3}{8}'' \times 2\frac{1}{2}''$ ROUND FRONT EDGE $\frac{1}{4}''$ RADIUS

ANDREW'S EASEL

This is a terrific activity center for several children at the same time. One side has a chalkboard and cabinet for chalk supplies, while the other has a paper holder for painting or sketching, an erasable marker board, a fold-down desk, and another cabinet for paint supplies. Its extension legs allow it to grow with the child. Size: 30" wide, 47" high, 31" deep, open.

ANDREW'S EASEL

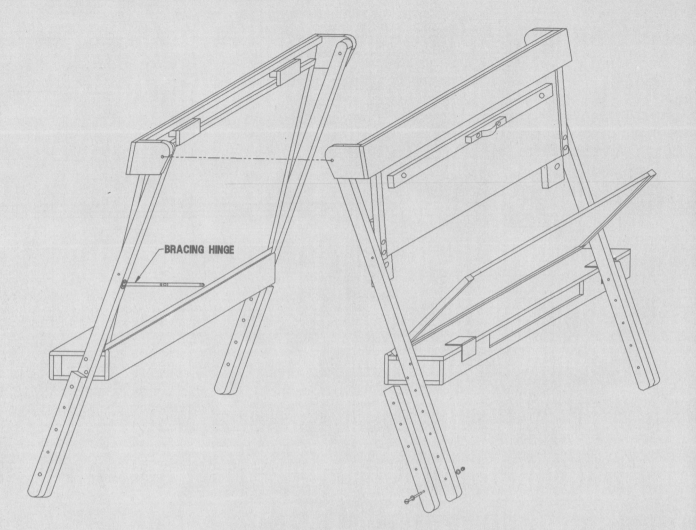

BRACING HINGE

ITEMS THAT CAN BE PURCHASED FROM
SUN DESIGNS
    PAINT CAKES WITH CONTAINERS
    WATER BOTTLES WITH CAPS
    ERASABLE MARKING SURFACE
    DECAL OF NUMBERS AND ALPHABET
    DECORATIVE HIGH BACK HINGES
    FULL SIZE DRAWINGS

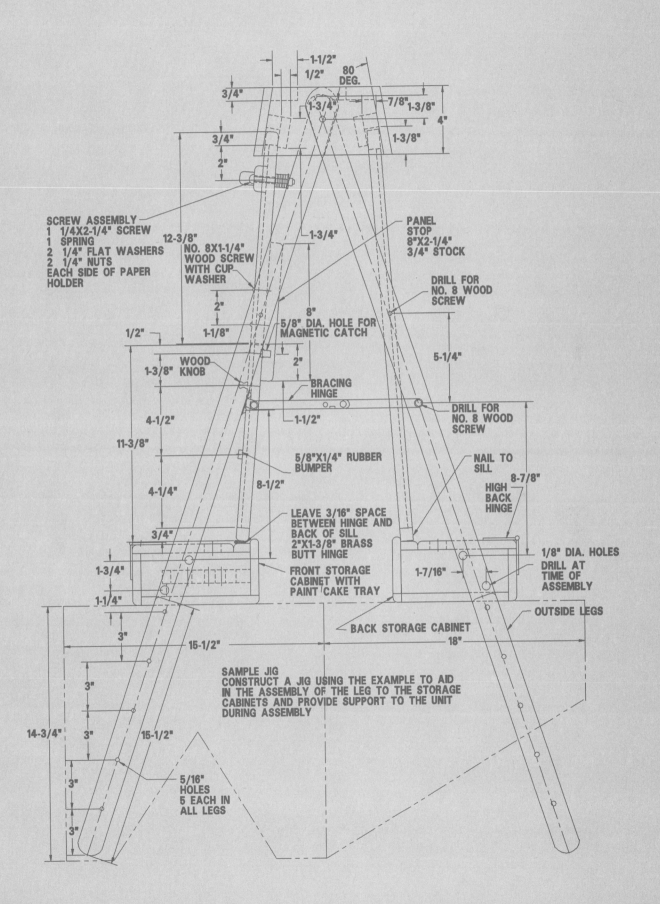

SCREW ASSEMBLY
1 1/4X2-1/4" SCREW
1 SPRING
2 1/4" FLAT WASHERS
2 1/4" NUTS
EACH SIDE OF PAPER
HOLDER

NO. 8X1-1/4"
WOOD SCREW
WITH CUP
WASHER

5/8" DIA. HOLE FOR
MAGNETIC CATCH

WOOD
KNOB

BRACING
HINGE

5/8"X1/4" RUBBER
BUMPER

LEAVE 3/16" SPACE
BETWEEN HINGE AND
BACK OF SILL
2"X1-3/8" BRASS
BUTT HINGE

FRONT STORAGE
CABINET WITH
PAINT CAKE TRAY

BACK STORAGE CABINET

PANEL
STOP
8"X2-1/4"
3/4" STOCK

DRILL FOR
NO. 8 WOOD
SCREW

DRILL FOR
NO. 8 WOOD
SCREW

NAIL TO
SILL

HIGH
BACK
HINGE

1/8" DIA. HOLES
DRILL AT
TIME OF
ASSEMBLY

OUTSIDE LEGS

SAMPLE JIG
CONSTRUCT A JIG USING THE EXAMPLE TO AID
IN THE ASSEMBLY OF THE LEG TO THE STORAGE
CABINETS AND PROVIDE SUPPORT TO THE UNIT
DURING ASSEMBLY

5/16"
HOLES
5 EACH IN
ALL LEGS

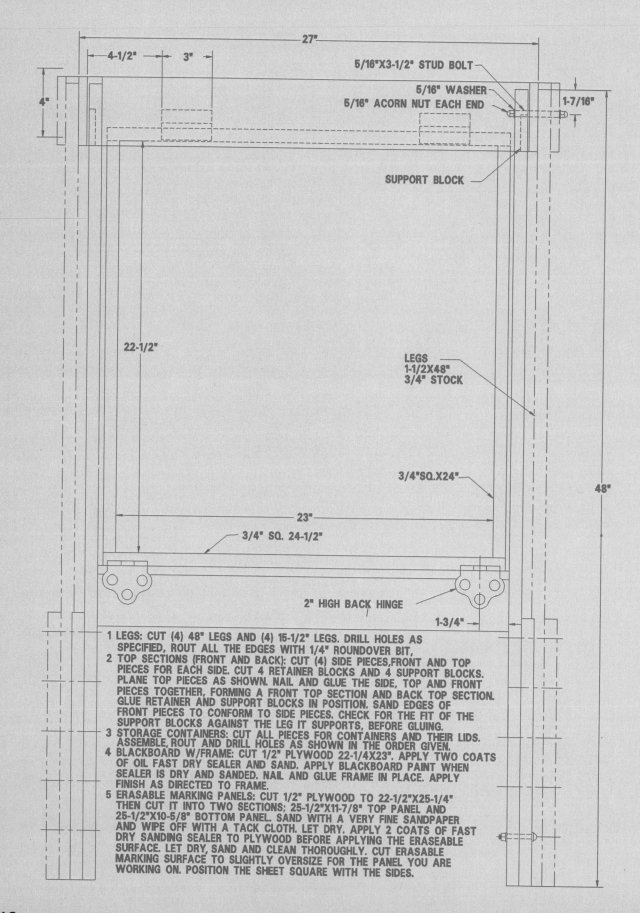

27"

4-1/2"   3"

5/16"X3-1/2" STUD BOLT

5/16" WASHER

5/16" ACORN NUT EACH END

4"

1-7/16"

SUPPORT BLOCK

22-1/2"

LEGS
1-1/2X48"
3/4" STOCK

3/4"SQ.X24"

23"

3/4" SQ. 24-1/2"

2" HIGH BACK HINGE

1-3/4"

48"

1 LEGS: CUT (4) 48" LEGS AND (4) 15-1/2" LEGS. DRILL HOLES AS
  SPECIFIED, ROUT ALL THE EDGES WITH 1/4" ROUNDOVER BIT,
2 TOP SECTIONS (FRONT AND BACK): CUT (4) SIDE PIECES,FRONT AND TOP
  PIECES FOR EACH SIDE. CUT 4 RETAINER BLOCKS AND 4 SUPPORT BLOCKS.
  PLANE TOP PIECES AS SHOWN. NAIL AND GLUE THE SIDE, TOP AND FRONT
  PIECES TOGETHER, FORMING A FRONT TOP SECTION AND BACK TOP SECTION.
  GLUE RETAINER AND SUPPORT BLOCKS IN POSITION. SAND EDGES OF
  FRONT PIECES TO CONFORM TO SIDE PIECES. CHECK FOR THE FIT OF THE
  SUPPORT BLOCKS AGAINST THE LEG IT SUPPORTS, BEFORE GLUING.
3 STORAGE CONTAINERS: CUT ALL PIECES FOR CONTAINERS AND THEIR LIDS.
  ASSEMBLE, ROUT AND DRILL HOLES AS SHOWN IN THE ORDER GIVEN.
4 BLACKBOARD W/FRAME: CUT 1/2" PLYWOOD 22-1/4X23". APPLY TWO COATS
  OF OIL FAST DRY SEALER AND SAND. APPLY BLACKBOARD PAINT WHEN
  SEALER IS DRY AND SANDED. NAIL AND GLUE FRAME IN PLACE. APPLY
  FINISH AS DIRECTED TO FRAME.
5 ERASABLE MARKING PANELS: CUT 1/2" PLYWOOD TO 22-1/2"X25-1/4"
  THEN CUT IT INTO TWO SECTIONS; 25-1/2"X11-7/8" TOP PANEL AND
  25-1/2"X10-5/8" BOTTOM PANEL. SAND WITH A VERY FINE SANDPAPER
  AND WIPE OFF WITH A TACK CLOTH. LET DRY. APPLY 2 COATS OF FAST
  DRY SANDING SEALER TO PLYWOOD BEFORE APPLYING THE ERASEABLE
  SURFACE. LET DRY, SAND AND CLEAN THOROUGHLY. CUT ERASABLE
  MARKING SURFACE TO SLIGHTLY OVERSIZE FOR THE PANEL YOU ARE
  WORKING ON. POSITION THE SHEET SQUARE WITH THE SIDES.

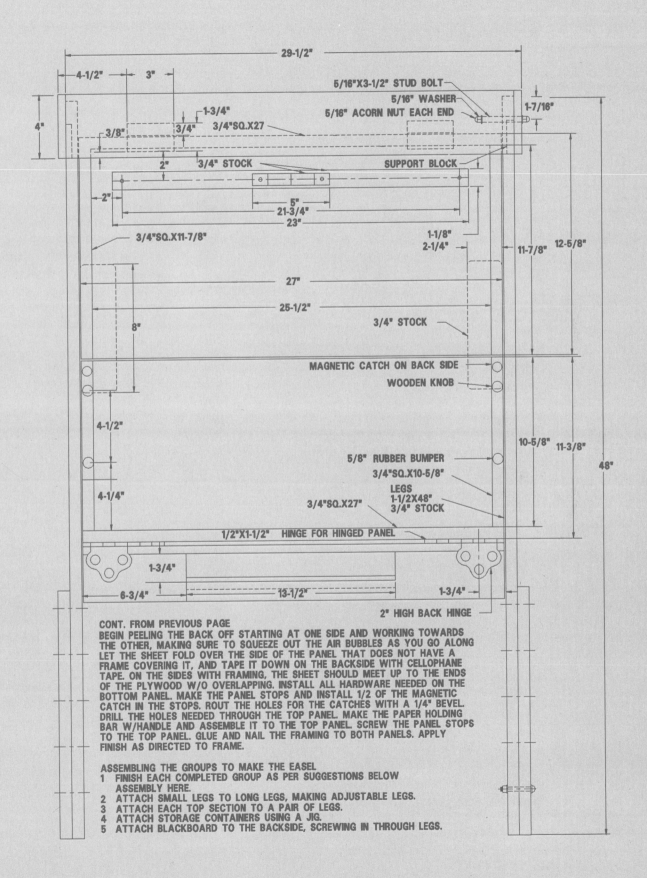

29-1/2"

4-1/2" 3"

5/16"X3-1/2" STUD BOLT
5/16" WASHER
5/16" ACORN NUT EACH END

1-7/16"

4"

1-3/4"

3/8" 3/4" 3/4"SQ.X27

2" 3/4" STOCK

SUPPORT BLOCK

2"

5"
21-3/4"
23"

3/4"SQ.X11-7/8"

1-1/8"
2-1/4"

11-7/8" 12-5/8"

27"

25-1/2"

8" 3/4" STOCK

MAGNETIC CATCH ON BACK SIDE

WOODEN KNOB

4-1/2"

5/8" RUBBER BUMPER
3/4"SQ.X10-5/8"

10-5/8" 11-3/8"

48"

4-1/4"

LEGS
1-1/2X48"
3/4" STOCK

3/4"SQ.X27"

1/2"X1-1/2" HINGE FOR HINGED PANEL

1-3/4"

6-3/4" 13-1/2" 1-3/4"

2" HIGH BACK HINGE

CONT. FROM PREVIOUS PAGE
BEGIN PEELING THE BACK OFF STARTING AT ONE SIDE AND WORKING TOWARDS
THE OTHER, MAKING SURE TO SQUEEZE OUT THE AIR BUBBLES AS YOU GO ALONG
LET THE SHEET FOLD OVER THE SIDE OF THE PANEL THAT DOES NOT HAVE A
FRAME COVERING IT, AND TAPE IT DOWN ON THE BACKSIDE WITH CELLOPHANE
TAPE. ON THE SIDES WITH FRAMING, THE SHEET SHOULD MEET UP TO THE ENDS
OF THE PLYWOOD W/O OVERLAPPING. INSTALL ALL HARDWARE NEEDED ON THE
BOTTOM PANEL. MAKE THE PANEL STOPS AND INSTALL 1/2 OF THE MAGNETIC
CATCH IN THE STOPS. ROUT THE HOLES FOR THE CATCHES WITH A 1/4" BEVEL.
DRILL THE HOLES NEEDED THROUGH THE TOP PANEL. MAKE THE PAPER HOLDING
BAR W/HANDLE AND ASSEMBLE IT TO THE TOP PANEL. SCREW THE PANEL STOPS
TO THE TOP PANEL. GLUE AND NAIL THE FRAMING TO BOTH PANELS. APPLY
FINISH AS DIRECTED TO FRAME.

ASSEMBLING THE GROUPS TO MAKE THE EASEL
1 FINISH EACH COMPLETED GROUP AS PER SUGGESTIONS BELOW
   ASSEMBLY HERE.
2 ATTACH SMALL LEGS TO LONG LEGS, MAKING ADJUSTABLE LEGS.
3 ATTACH EACH TOP SECTION TO A PAIR OF LEGS.
4 ATTACH STORAGE CONTAINERS USING A JIG.
5 ATTACH BLACKBOARD TO THE BACKSIDE, SCREWING IN THROUGH LEGS.

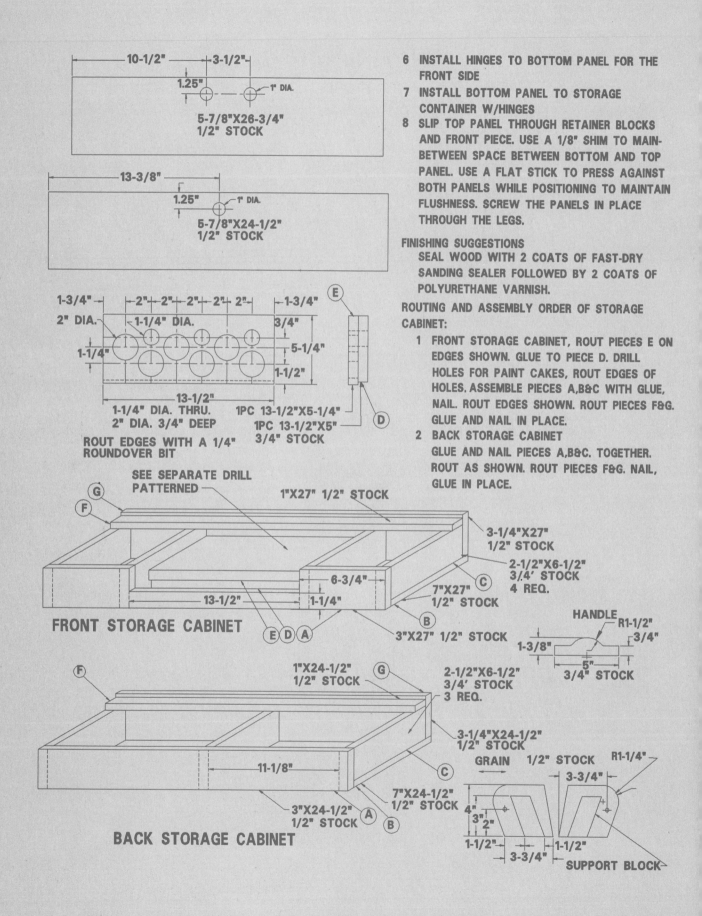

10-1/2" — 3-1/2"

1.25"

1" DIA.

5-7/8"X26-3/4"
1/2" STOCK

13-3/8"

1.25"   1" DIA.

5-7/8"X24-1/2"
1/2" STOCK

1-3/4" — 2" — 2" — 2" — 2" — 2" — 1-3/4"

E

2" DIA.

1-1/4" DIA.

3/4"

1-1/4"

5-1/4"

1-1/2"

13-1/2"

1-1/4" DIA. THRU.
2" DIA. 3/4" DEEP

1PC 13-1/2"X5-1/4"

1PC 13-1/2"X5"
3/4" STOCK

ROUT EDGES WITH A 1/4"
ROUNDOVER BIT

D

SEE SEPARATE DRILL
PATTERNED

1"X27" 1/2" STOCK

G

F

3-1/4"X27"
1/2" STOCK

2-1/2"X6-1/2"
3/4' STOCK
4 REQ.

C

6-3/4"

13-1/2"   1-1/4"

7"X27"
1/2" STOCK

FRONT STORAGE CABINET

E D A

B

3"X27" 1/2" STOCK

1"X24-1/2"
1/2" STOCK

G

2-1/2"X6-1/2"
3/4' STOCK
3 REQ.

3-1/4"X24-1/2"
1/2" STOCK

F

11-1/8"

C

7"X24-1/2"
1/2" STOCK

3"X24-1/2"
1/2" STOCK

A

B

BACK STORAGE CABINET

HANDLE

R1-1/2"

3/4"

1-3/8"

5"

3/4" STOCK

GRAIN   1/2" STOCK   R1-1/4"

3-3/4"

4"

3"   2"

1-1/2"   1-1/2"

3-3/4"

SUPPORT BLOCK

6 INSTALL HINGES TO BOTTOM PANEL FOR THE
FRONT SIDE

7 INSTALL BOTTOM PANEL TO STORAGE
CONTAINER W/HINGES

8 SLIP TOP PANEL THROUGH RETAINER BLOCKS
AND FRONT PIECE. USE A 1/8" SHIM TO MAIN-
BETWEEN SPACE BETWEEN BOTTOM AND TOP
PANEL. USE A FLAT STICK TO PRESS AGAINST
BOTH PANELS WHILE POSITIONING TO MAINTAIN
FLUSHNESS. SCREW THE PANELS IN PLACE
THROUGH THE LEGS.

FINISHING SUGGESTIONS
SEAL WOOD WITH 2 COATS OF FAST-DRY
SANDING SEALER FOLLOWED BY 2 COATS OF
POLYURETHANE VARNISH.

ROUTING AND ASSEMBLY ORDER OF STORAGE
CABINET:

1 FRONT STORAGE CABINET, ROUT PIECES E ON
EDGES SHOWN. GLUE TO PIECE D. DRILL
HOLES FOR PAINT CAKES, ROUT EDGES OF
HOLES. ASSEMBLE PIECES A,B&C WITH GLUE,
NAIL. ROUT EDGES SHOWN. ROUT PIECES F&G.
GLUE AND NAIL IN PLACE.

2 BACK STORAGE CABINET
GLUE AND NAIL PIECES A,B&C. TOGETHER.
ROUT AS SHOWN. ROUT PIECES F&G. NAIL,
GLUE IN PLACE.

THE VIKING

Imagine yourself on the custom cushion snugly blanketed—
with warm snacks riding in the rear rumbleseat com-
partment. You are gliding swiftly over the glistening moonlit
snow, under full power with your favorite reindeer (second
power choice—Mom or Dad). Size: 43″ long, 23″ high, 21″ wide.

THE VIKING

ROUT ALL EDGES WITH 1/4" ROUND OVER BIT WHERE POSSIBLE

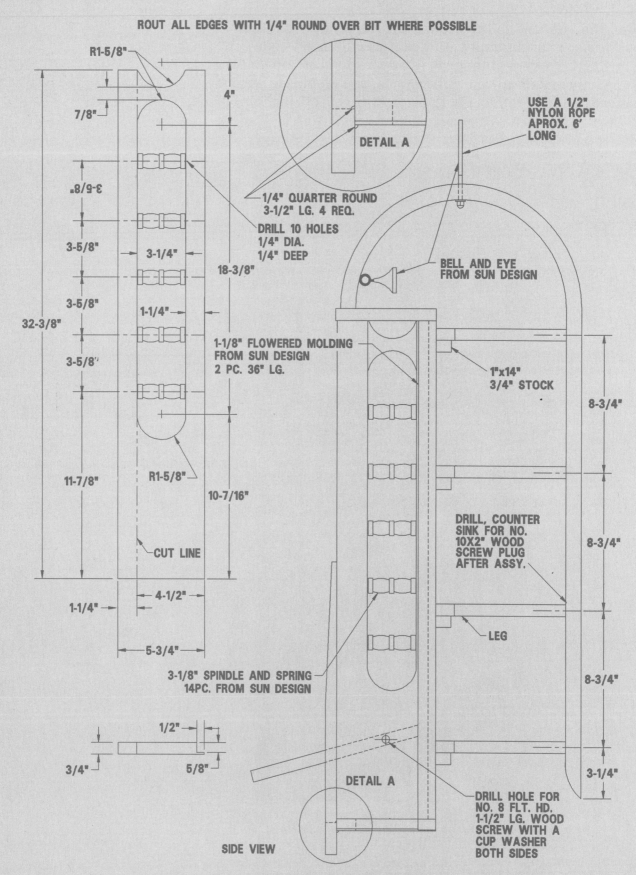

R1-5/8"

4"

7/8"

DETAIL A

USE A 1/2"
NYLON ROPE
APROX. 6'
LONG

1/4" QUARTER ROUND
3-1/2" LG. 4 REQ.

DRILL 10 HOLES
1/4" DIA.
1/4" DEEP

3-5/8"

3-5/8"

3-1/4"

18-3/8"

BELL AND EYE
FROM SUN DESIGN

3-5/8"

1-1/4"

1"x14"
3/4" STOCK

8-3/4"

1-1/8" FLOWERED MOLDING
FROM SUN DESIGN
2 PC. 36" LG.

32-3/8"

3-5/8"

R1-5/8"

DRILL, COUNTER
SINK FOR NO.
10X2" WOOD
SCREW PLUG
AFTER ASSY.

8-3/4"

11-7/8"

10-7/16"

CUT LINE

LEG

4-1/2"

1-1/4"

8-3/4"

5-3/4"

3-1/8" SPINDLE AND SPRING
14PC. FROM SUN DESIGN

1/2"

3/4"

5/8"

DETAIL A

3-1/4"

DRILL HOLE FOR
NO. 8 FLT. HD.
1-1/2" LG. WOOD
SCREW WITH A
CUP WASHER
BOTH SIDES

SIDE VIEW

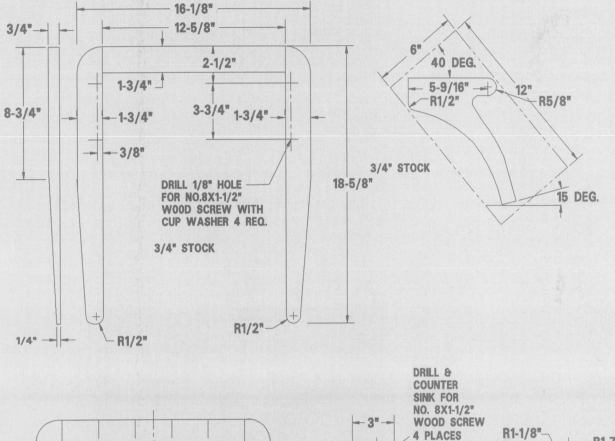

16-1/8"

12-5/8"

3/4"

2-1/2"

1-3/4"

1-3/4"

8-3/4"

1-3/4"

3-3/4" 1-3/4"

3/8"

6"

40 DEG.

5-9/16"

R1/2"

12"

R5/8"

3/4" STOCK

15 DEG.

DRILL 1/8" HOLE
FOR NO.8X1-1/2"
WOOD SCREW WITH
CUP WASHER 4 REQ.

18-5/8"

3/4" STOCK

1/4"

R1/2"

R1/2"

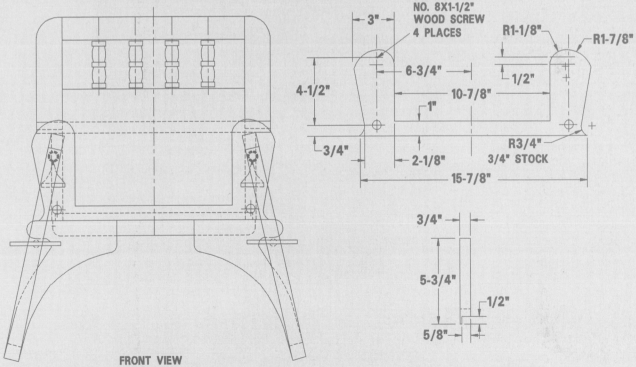

DRILL &
COUNTER
SINK FOR
NO. 8X1-1/2"
WOOD SCREW
4 PLACES

3"

R1-1/8"

R1-7/8"

6-3/4"

4-1/2"

1/2"

10-7/8"

1"

3/4"

2-1/8"

R3/4"

3/4" STOCK

15-7/8"

3/4"

5-3/4"

1/2"

5/8"

FRONT VIEW

ROUT ALL EDGES WITH 1/4" ROUND OVER BIT WHERE POSSIBLE

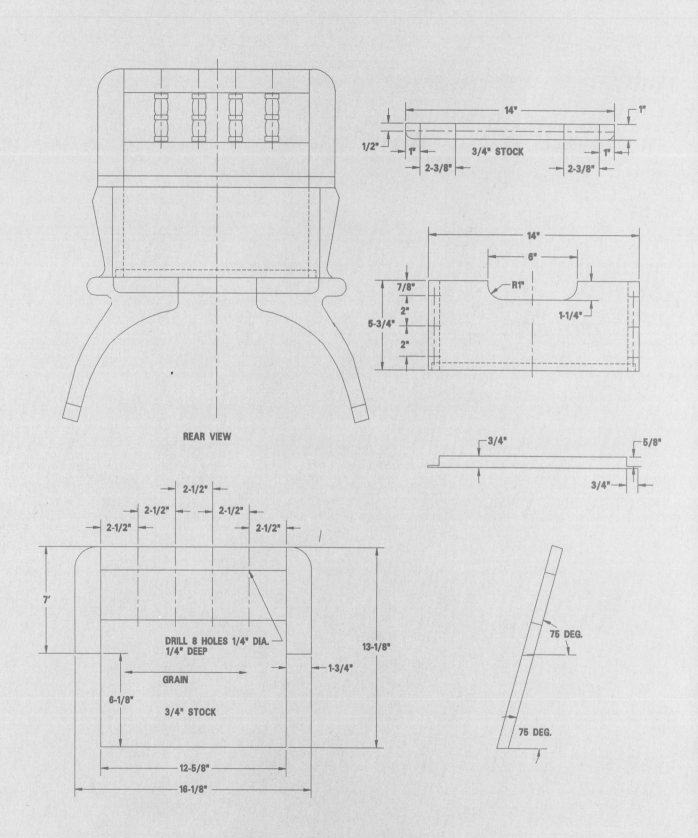

REAR VIEW

14"

1"

1/2"

1"

3/4" STOCK

2-3/8"

1"

2-3/8"

14"

6"

7/8"

R1"

2"

5-3/4"

1-1/4"

2"

3/4"

5/8"

3/4"

2-1/2"

2-1/2"

2-1/2"

2-1/2"

2-1/2"

7'

DRILL 8 HOLES 1/4" DIA.
1/4" DEEP

13-1/8"

GRAIN

1-3/4"

6-1/8"

3/4" STOCK

12-5/8"

16-1/8"

75 DEG.

75 DEG.

ROUT ALL EDGES WITH 1/4" ROUND OVER BIT WHERE POSSIBLE

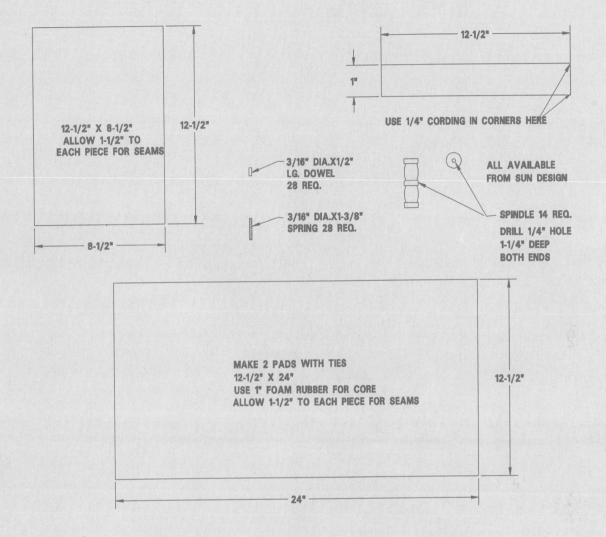

12-1/2" X 8-1/2"
ALLOW 1-1/2" TO
EACH PIECE FOR SEAMS

12-1/2"

8-1/2"

12-1/2"

1"

USE 1/4" CORDING IN CORNERS HERE

3/16" DIA.X1/2"
LG. DOWEL
28 REQ.

3/16" DIA.X1-3/8"
SPRING 28 REQ.

ALL AVAILABLE
FROM SUN DESIGN

SPINDLE 14 REQ.

DRILL 1/4" HOLE
1-1/4" DEEP
BOTH ENDS

MAKE 2 PADS WITH TIES
12-1/2" X 24"
USE 1" FOAM RUBBER FOR CORE
ALLOW 1-1/2" TO EACH PIECE FOR SEAMS

12-1/2"

24"

FLOOR
1/2" PLYWOOD OR SOLID STOCK

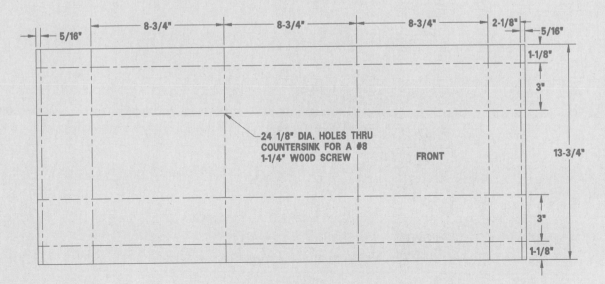

5/16"

8-3/4"

8-3/4"

8-3/4"

2-1/8"

5/16"

1-1/8"

3"

24 1/8" DIA. HOLES THRU
COUNTERSINK FOR A #8
1-1/4" WOOD SCREW

FRONT

13-3/4"

3"

1-1/8"

DUMP TRUCK
An old-fashioned wooden dump truck that has a positive dump action and a swivel-opening tailgate with brass latch. It's sized to work with all the other construction toys. Size: 19″ long, 8″ wide.

STEAM SHOVEL
A nice-sized toy to teach coordination. The right side crank moves bucket up and down. The left side crank moves bucket forward and backward. The cab swivels on its base, giving unlimited digging and dumping action. Has a simple and effective springloaded dump action. Size: 12" long, 17" high.

DUMP TRUCK

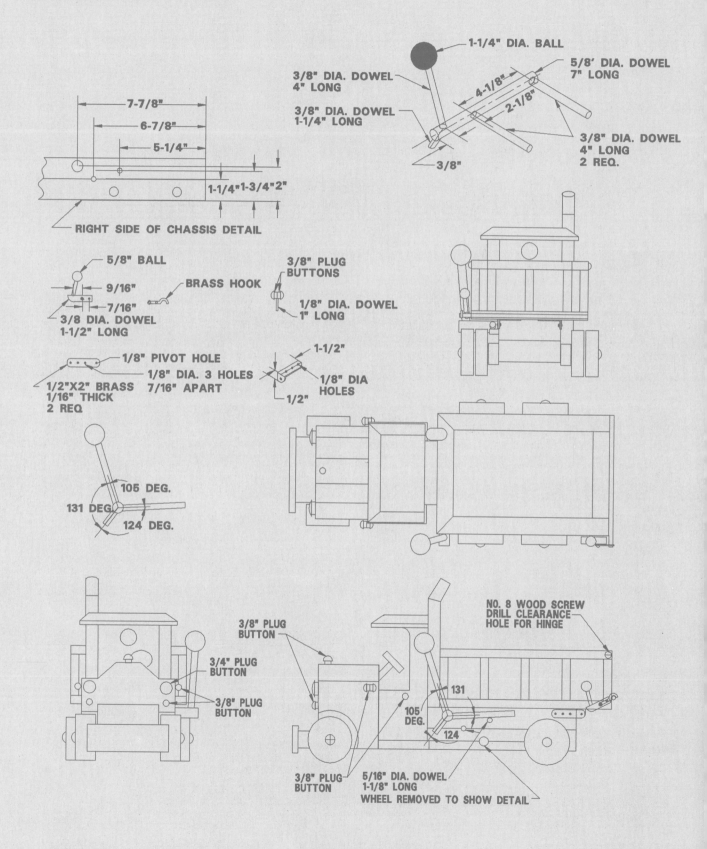

RIGHT SIDE OF CHASSIS DETAIL

7-7/8"
6-7/8"
5-1/4"
1-1/4" 1-3/4" 2"

1-1/4" DIA. BALL
3/8" DIA. DOWEL 4" LONG
3/8" DIA. DOWEL 1-1/4" LONG
5/8' DIA. DOWEL 7" LONG
4-1/8"
2-1/8"
3/8" DIA. DOWEL 4" LONG 2 REQ.
3/8"

5/8" BALL
9/16"
7/16"
3/8 DIA. DOWEL 1-1/2" LONG
BRASS HOOK
3/8" PLUG BUTTONS
1/8" DIA. DOWEL 1" LONG

1/8" PIVOT HOLE
1/8" DIA. 3 HOLES 7/16" APART
1/2"X2" BRASS 1/16" THICK 2 REQ
1-1/2"
1/8" DIA HOLES
1/2"

105 DEG.
131 DEG.
124 DEG.

NO. 8 WOOD SCREW DRILL CLEARANCE HOLE FOR HINGE

3/8" PLUG BUTTON
3/4" PLUG BUTTON
3/8" PLUG BUTTON

3/8" PLUG BUTTON

131
105 DEG.
124

3/8" PLUG BUTTON
5/16" DIA. DOWEL 1-1/8" LONG
WHEEL REMOVED TO SHOW DETAIL

22

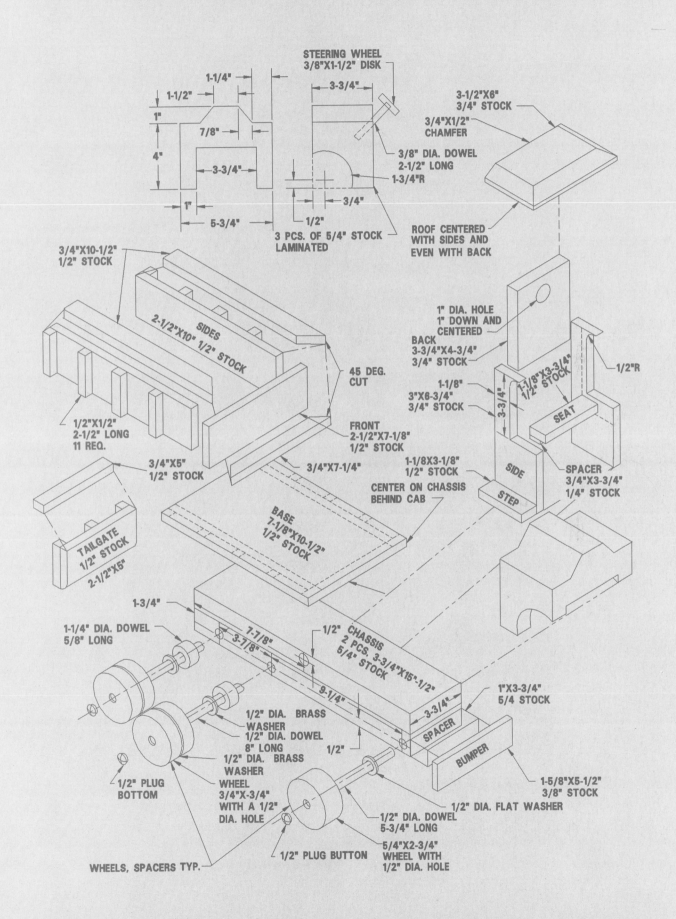

STEERING WHEEL
3/8"X1-1/2" DISK

1-1/4"
1-1/2"
1"
7/8"
4"
3-3/4"
1"
5-3/4"

3-3/4"
3/8" DIA. DOWEL
2-1/2" LONG
1-3/4"R
3/4"
1/2"

3 PCS. OF 5/4" STOCK
LAMINATED

3-1/2"X6"
3/4" STOCK

3/4"X1/2"
CHAMFER

ROOF CENTERED
WITH SIDES AND
EVEN WITH BACK

3/4"X10-1/2"
1/2" STOCK

SIDES

2-1/2"X10" 1/2" STOCK

45 DEG.
CUT

1" DIA. HOLE
1" DOWN AND
CENTERED

BACK
3-3/4"X4-3/4"
3/4" STOCK

1-1/8"X3-3/4"
1/2" STOCK

1/2"R

1-1/8"
3"X6-3/4"
3/4" STOCK

3-3/4"

SEAT

SIDE

SPACER
3/4"X3-3/4"
1/4" STOCK

1/2"X1/2"
2-1/2" LONG
11 REQ.

3/4"X5"
1/2" STOCK

3/4"X7-1/4"

FRONT
2-1/2"X7-1/8"
1/2" STOCK

1-1/8X3-1/8"
1/2" STOCK

CENTER ON CHASSIS
BEHIND CAB

STEP

TAILGATE
1/2" STOCK

2-1/2"X5"

BASE
7-1/8"X10-1/2"
1/2" STOCK

1-3/4"

1-1/4" DIA. DOWEL
5/8" LONG

7-7/8"
3-7/8"

1/2" CHASSIS
2 PCS. 3-3/4"X15-1/2"
5/4" STOCK

9-1/4"

3-3/4"

1"X3-3/4"
5/4 STOCK

SPACER

1/2" DIA. BRASS
WASHER
1/2" DIA. DOWEL
8" LONG
1/2" DIA. BRASS
WASHER

WHEEL
3/4"X3-3/4"
WITH A 1/2"
DIA. HOLE

1/2"

BUMPER

1-5/8"X5-1/2"
3/8" STOCK

1/2" PLUG
BOTTOM

1/2" PLUG BUTTON

1/2" DIA. DOWEL
5-3/4" LONG

1/2" DIA. FLAT WASHER

5/4"X2-3/4"
WHEEL WITH
1/2" DIA. HOLE

WHEELS, SPACERS TYP.

23

STEAM SHOVEL

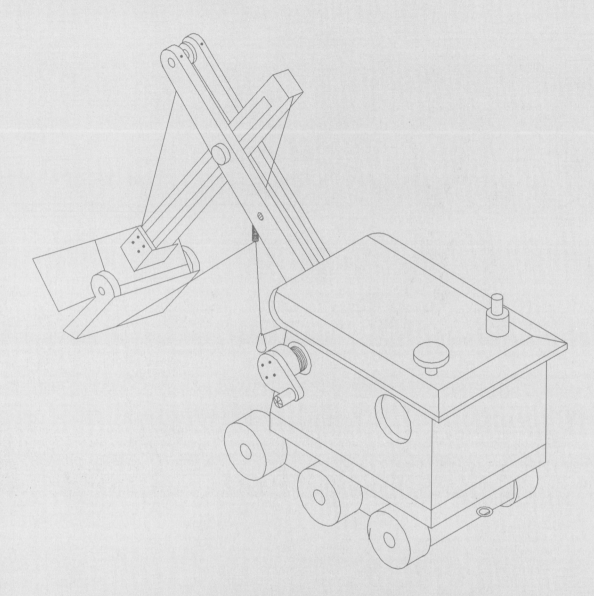

NOTE:
BOTH GEAR AXLE AND CRANK ASSEMBLIES HAVE THE SAME DIMENSIONS
AND HARDWARE THROUGHOUT.

START CONSTRUCTION OF TRACTOR BASE BY LAMINATING TWO PIECES
OF 2"X6" STOCK TOGETHER.

WHEELS ARE CUT FROM 2"X6" STOCK USING A HOLE CUTTER. DRILL A SMALL
PILOT HOLE FIRST. THIS WILL AID LATER IN DRILLING THE 9/16" DIA.
CENTER HOLE.

BE SURE TO DRILL AXLE AND WHEEL HOLES STRAIGHT, OTHERWISE
PROPER WHEEL ROTATION WILL BE AFFECTED.

THE SPRINGS USED IN THIS PROJECT ARE AVAILABLE DIRECTLY FROM
SUN DESIGNS AS AN ACCESSORY HARDWARE PACKAGE.

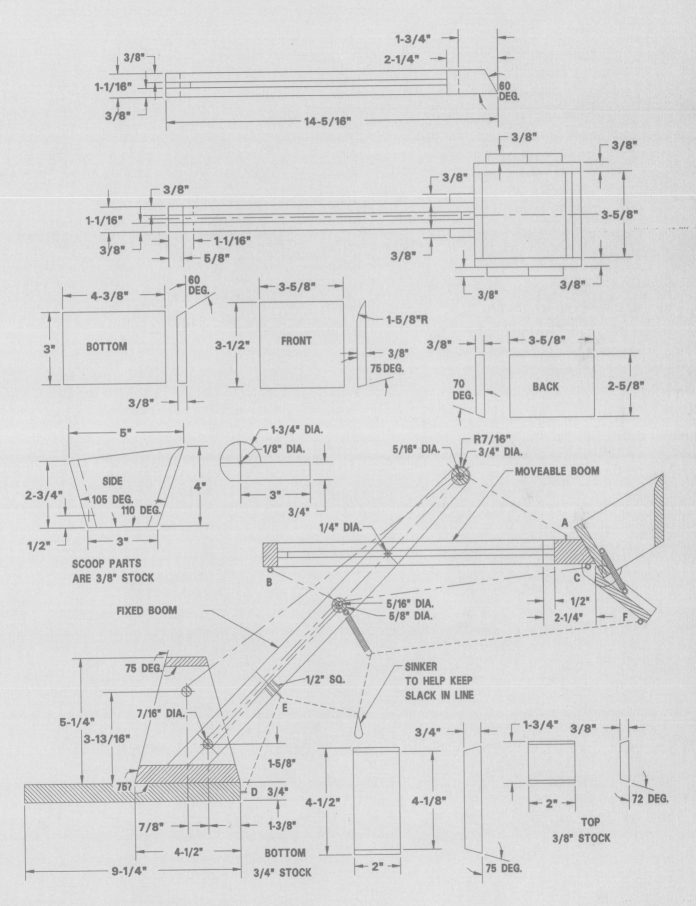

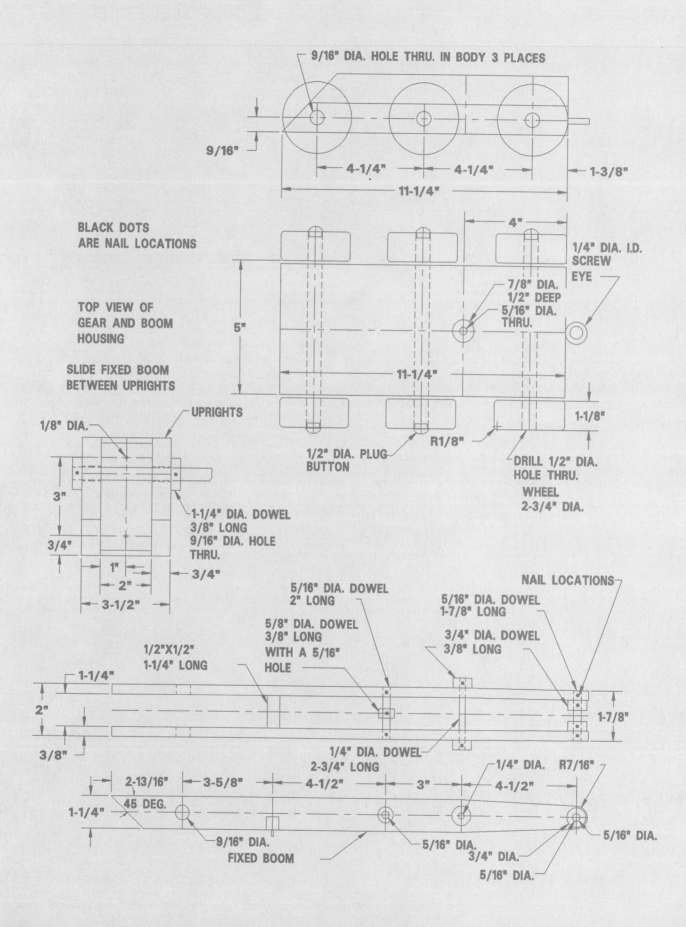

9/16" DIA. HOLE THRU. IN BODY 3 PLACES

9/16"

4-1/4"   4-1/4"   1-3/8"

11-1/4"

BLACK DOTS
ARE NAIL LOCATIONS

4"

1/4" DIA. I.D.
SCREW
EYE

TOP VIEW OF
GEAR AND BOOM
HOUSING

7/8" DIA.
1/2" DEEP
5/16" DIA.
THRU.

5"

SLIDE FIXED BOOM
BETWEEN UPRIGHTS

11-1/4"

1-1/8"

UPRIGHTS

1/8" DIA.

1/2" DIA. PLUG
BUTTON

R1/8"

DRILL 1/2" DIA.
HOLE THRU.

3"

WHEEL
2-3/4" DIA.

1-1/4" DIA. DOWEL
3/8" LONG
9/16" DIA. HOLE
THRU.

3/4"

1"   3/4"

2"

3-1/2"

NAIL LOCATIONS

5/16" DIA. DOWEL
2" LONG

5/16" DIA. DOWEL
1-7/8" LONG

5/8" DIA. DOWEL
3/8" LONG
WITH A 5/16"
HOLE

3/4" DIA. DOWEL
3/8" LONG

1/2"X1/2"
1-1/4" LONG

1-1/4"

2"

1-7/8"

3/8"

1/4" DIA. DOWEL
2-3/4" LONG

2-13/16"   3-5/8"   4-1/2"   3"   4-1/2"

1/4" DIA.   R7/16"

1-1/4"   45 DEG.

9/16" DIA.
FIXED BOOM

5/16" DIA.

3/4" DIA.

5/16" DIA.

5/16" DIA.

26

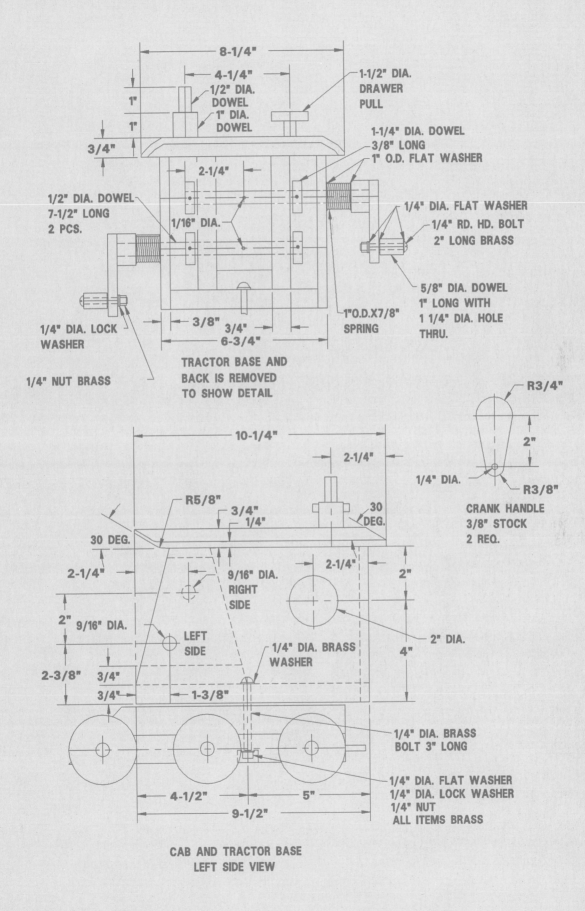

8-1/4"
4-1/4"
1/2" DIA. DOWEL
1" DIA. DOWEL
1"
1"
3/4"

1-1/2" DIA. DRAWER PULL

1-1/4" DIA. DOWEL
3/8" LONG
1" O.D. FLAT WASHER

2-1/4"

1/2" DIA. DOWEL
7-1/2" LONG
2 PCS.

1/16" DIA.

1/4" DIA. FLAT WASHER

1/4" RD. HD. BOLT
2" LONG BRASS

5/8" DIA. DOWEL
1" LONG WITH
1 1/4" DIA. HOLE THRU.

1/4" DIA. LOCK WASHER

3/8"
3/4"
6-3/4"

1"O.D.X7/8" SPRING

1/4" NUT BRASS

TRACTOR BASE AND BACK IS REMOVED TO SHOW DETAIL

R3/4"
2"
1/4" DIA.
R3/8"

**CRANK HANDLE
3/8" STOCK
2 REQ.**

10-1/4"
2-1/4"

R5/8"
3/4"
1/4"
30 DEG.

30 DEG.
2-1/4"

9/16" DIA. RIGHT SIDE

2-1/4"
2"

2" 9/16" DIA.

LEFT SIDE

1/4" DIA. BRASS WASHER

2" DIA.

4"

2-3/8"
3/4"
3/4"
1-3/8"

1/4" DIA. BRASS BOLT 3" LONG

1/4" DIA. FLAT WASHER
1/4" DIA. LOCK WASHER
1/4" NUT
ALL ITEMS BRASS

4-1/2"
5"
9-1/2"

**CAB AND TRACTOR BASE
LEFT SIDE VIEW**

NOTES:

THE STEAM SHOVEL CONSISTS OF FOUR SUB ASSEMBLIES: CAB, TRACTOR BASE, FIXED BOOM AND GEAR HOUSING, AND THE MOVABLE SHOVEL BOOM.

CONSTRUCTION OF THESE ASSEMBLIES CAN BE IN ANY ORDER. HOWEVER, IN BUILDING THE CAB DO NOT PUT THE TOP ON UNTIL ALL GEAR ASSEMBLIES ARE IN PLACE AND STRUNG.

STUDY CAREFULLY HOW THE GEARS AND BOOMS ARE STRUNG.

THE TOP GEAR IMPARTS VERTICAL MOTION TO THE SHOVEL BOOM. IT IS STRUNG AS FOLLOWS: CUT A 2' LENGTH OF CHALK LINE CORD. PASS ONE END THRU 1/16" DIA. HOLE IN UPPER GEAR AXLE AND TIE IT OFF. RUN LINE AS SHOWN OVER TOP DOWEL BRIDGE OF FIXED BOOM AND TIE OFF OTHER END AT EYELET A.

THE BOTTOM GEAR IMPARTS HORIZONTAL MOTION TO THE SHOVEL BOOM. STRING AS FOLLOWS: CUT A 3-1/2' LENGTH OF CHALK LINE CORD. PASS ONE END THRU 1/16" DIA. HOLE IN LOWER GEAR AXLE, WRAP SEVERAL TIMES, THEN RUN LINE AS SHOWN (PHANTOM LINES) AND TIE OFF AT EYELET B. TAKE THE OTHER END AND WRAP AROUND AXLE IN THE OPPOSITE DIRECTION, RUN LINE AS SHOWN (DASHED LINE) ALLOW SLACK AND TIE OFF AT EYELET C

BOTTOM OF SCOOP OPENS TO DUMP CONTENTS AS SHOWN. STRING AS FOLLOWS: CUT 2' LENGTH OF CHALK LINE CORD, TIE OFF END AT EYELET D. PASS THE OTHER END THRU EYELET E. THEN THRU SINKER EYELET AND TIE OFF AT F. CONNECT SPRING AS SHOWN.

TEST ALL MOVABLE PARTS FOR FREEDOM OF FIT. ASSEMBLE ONLY WHEN PARTS FIT WITHOUT BINDING.

ANY PLACE WHERE FINISHING NAILS WERE USED, THE NAILS SHOULD BE SET USING A NAIL SET OF THE PROPER SIZE. PUTTY NAIL HOLES WHEN FINISHING.

BLACK DOTS ON DRAWING INDICATE PLACEMENT OF WIRE BRADS. USE NO LARGER THAN A #16 BRAD WHEN GOING THRU DOWEL PIECES SUCH AS SPACERS. USE NO LARGER THAN #18 BRADS THRU THIN PIECES THAT MIGHT SPLIT OTHERWISE. DRILL A PIN-HOLE FIRST BEFORE NAILING WITH WIRE BRADS.

CUT WINDOW HOLE IN SIDE PANELS OF CAB WITH A WOOD BLOCK UNDERNEATH TO PREVENT PANEL FROM SPLITTING.

THE WOOD SPACERS ARE CUT FROM THE APPROPRIATE DIAMETER DOWEL STOCK OR WITH A HOLE CUTTER WHERE NECESSARY.

SAND SURFACES AS NEEDED. NOTE THAT MOST EDGES ARE SANDED AND ROUNDED SLIGHTLY.
TO FINISH, USE TWO COATS OF SANDING SEALER, ONE COAT OF POLYURETHANE GLOSS VARNISH, SANDING BEFORE AND BETWEEN COATS.

PIN STRIPING SUPPLIES ARE READILY AVAILABLE AT MOST AUTO SUPPLY STORES.

READ ALL NOTES AND STUDY PLANS CAREFULLY BEFORE YOU BEGIN.

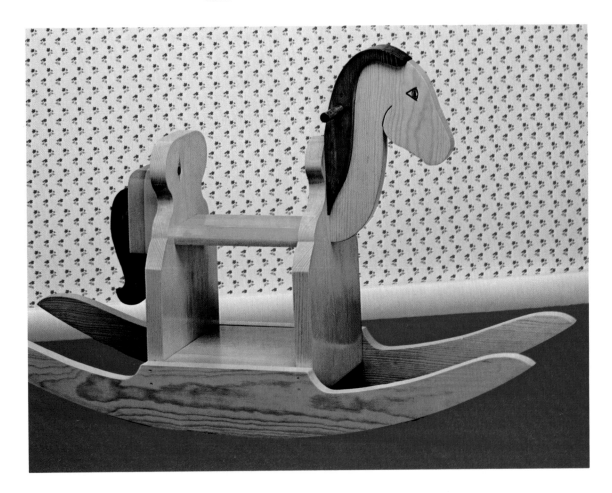

PRANCER (top)
Wouldn't any child love to ride this strutting horse? Included in plan are patterns for a bridle, stirrups, cushion, painted decoration. Size: 51″ long, 38″ high to top of head.

TUMBLEWEED (bottom)
A durable, all-wood rocking horse with a smooth, easy motion. Youngsters will like to crawl through it, and climb over it as much as they will like rocking on it. Size: 39″ long, 23″ high.

TUMBLEWEED

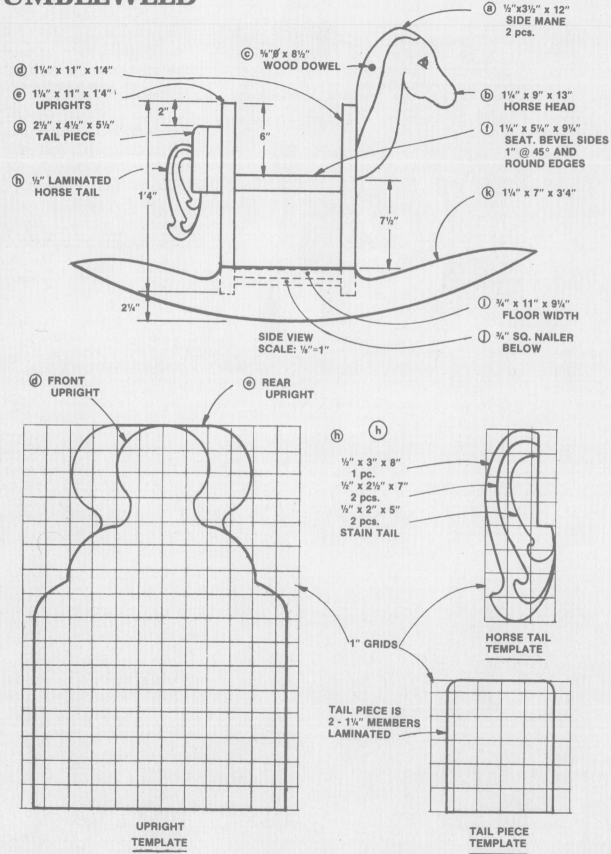

(a) ½"x3½" x 12"
SIDE MANE
2 pcs.

(c) ⅝"⌀ x 8½"
WOOD DOWEL

(d) 1¼" x 11" x 1'4"

(e) 1¼" x 11" x 1'4"
UPRIGHTS

(g) 2½" x 4½" x 5½"
TAIL PIECE

(h) ½" LAMINATED
HORSE TAIL

2"

6"

1'4"

7½"

2¼"

(b) 1¼" x 9" x 13"
HORSE HEAD

(f) 1¼" x 5¼" x 9¼"
SEAT. BEVEL SIDES
1" @ 45° AND
ROUND EDGES

(k) 1¼" x 7" x 3'4"

(i) ¾" x 11" x 9¼"
FLOOR WIDTH

(j) ¾" SQ. NAILER
BELOW

SIDE VIEW
SCALE: ⅛"=1"

(d) FRONT
UPRIGHT

(e) REAR
UPRIGHT

(h) (h)

½" x 3" x 8"
1 pc.
½" x 2½" x 7"
2 pcs.
½" x 2" x 5"
2 pcs.
STAIN TAIL

HORSE TAIL
TEMPLATE

1" GRIDS

TAIL PIECE IS
2 - 1¼" MEMBERS
LAMINATED

UPRIGHT
TEMPLATE

TAIL PIECE
TEMPLATE

PROCEDURE FOR HORSE'S HEAD

CUT OUT HEAD FROM 1¼" STOCK AND MANE FROM ½" STOCK AND GLUE (CLAMPED). NOTCH HEAD AND DRILL HOLE FOR DOWEL. GLUE DOWEL IN PLACE. STAIN MANE AND DOWEL.

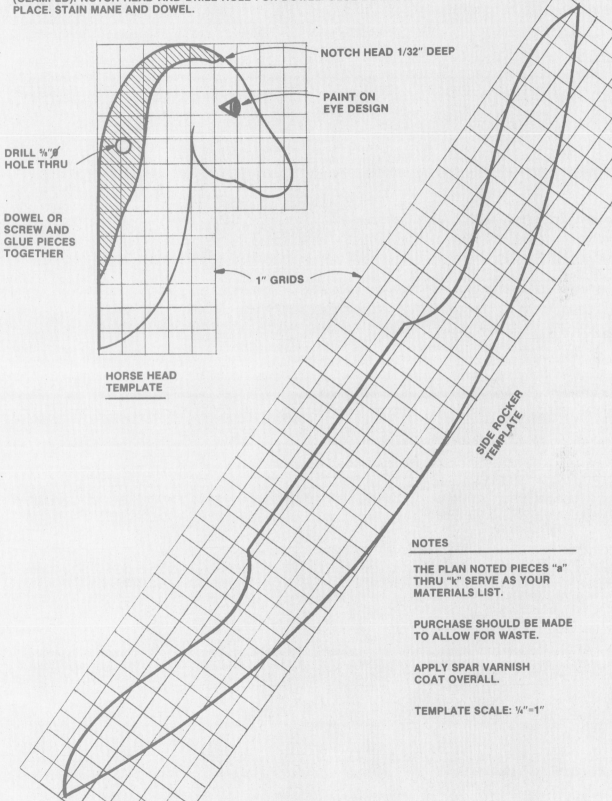

NOTCH HEAD 1/32" DEEP

PAINT ON EYE DESIGN

DRILL ⅝"∅ HOLE THRU

DOWEL OR SCREW AND GLUE PIECES TOGETHER

1" GRIDS

HORSE HEAD TEMPLATE

SIDE ROCKER TEMPLATE

NOTES

THE PLAN NOTED PIECES "a" THRU "k" SERVE AS YOUR MATERIALS LIST.

PURCHASE SHOULD BE MADE TO ALLOW FOR WASTE.

APPLY SPAR VARNISH COAT OVERALL.

TEMPLATE SCALE: ¼"=1"

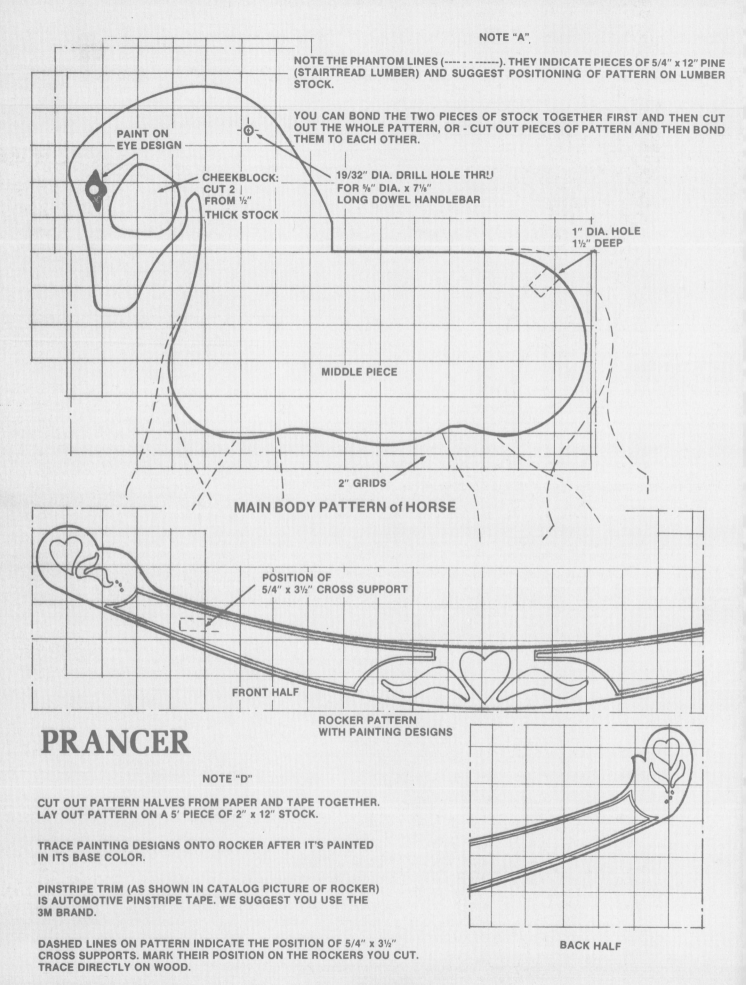

NOTE THE PHANTOM LINES (---- - ------). THEY INDICATE PIECES OF 5/4" x 12" PINE (STAIRTREAD LUMBER) AND SUGGEST POSITIONING OF PATTERN ON LUMBER STOCK.

YOU CAN BOND THE TWO PIECES OF STOCK TOGETHER FIRST AND THEN CUT OUT THE WHOLE PATTERN, OR - CUT OUT PIECES OF PATTERN AND THEN BOND THEM TO EACH OTHER.

PAINT ON
EYE DESIGN

CHEEKBLOCK:
CUT 2
FROM ½"
THICK STOCK

19/32" DIA. DRILL HOLE THRU
FOR ⅝" DIA. x 7⅛"
LONG DOWEL HANDLEBAR

1" DIA. HOLE
1½" DEEP

MIDDLE PIECE

2" GRIDS

MAIN BODY PATTERN of HORSE

POSITION OF
5/4" x 3½" CROSS SUPPORT

FRONT HALF

ROCKER PATTERN
WITH PAINTING DESIGNS

PRANCER

NOTE "D"

CUT OUT PATTERN HALVES FROM PAPER AND TAPE TOGETHER.
LAY OUT PATTERN ON A 5' PIECE OF 2" x 12" STOCK.

TRACE PAINTING DESIGNS ONTO ROCKER AFTER IT'S PAINTED
IN ITS BASE COLOR.

PINSTRIPE TRIM (AS SHOWN IN CATALOG PICTURE OF ROCKER)
IS AUTOMOTIVE PINSTRIPE TAPE. WE SUGGEST YOU USE THE
3M BRAND.

DASHED LINES ON PATTERN INDICATE THE POSITION OF 5/4" x 3½"
CROSS SUPPORTS. MARK THEIR POSITION ON THE ROCKERS YOU CUT.
TRACE DIRECTLY ON WOOD.

BACK HALF

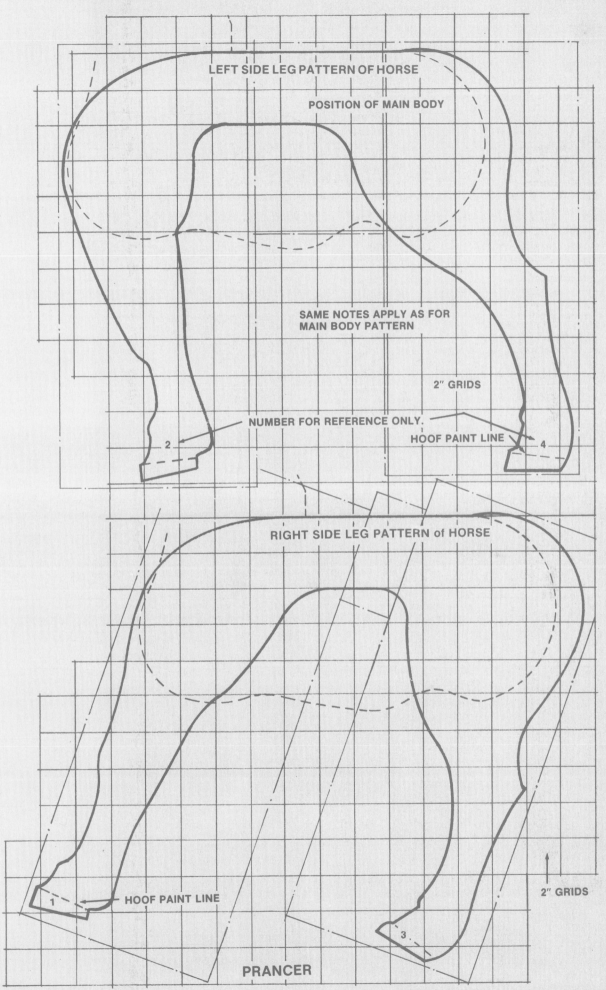

LEFT SIDE LEG PATTERN OF HORSE

POSITION OF MAIN BODY

SAME NOTES APPLY AS FOR
MAIN BODY PATTERN

2" GRIDS

NUMBER FOR REFERENCE ONLY.

HOOF PAINT LINE

2

4

RIGHT SIDE LEG PATTERN of HORSE

HOOF PAINT LINE

1

3

2" GRIDS

PRANCER

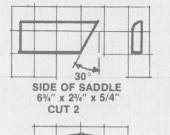

SIDE OF SADDLE
6¾" x 2¾" x 5/4"
CUT 2

30°

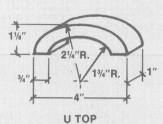

U TOP
CUT 2

1⅛"
2¼"R.
1¾"R.
¾"
1"
4"

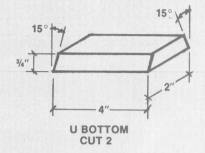

15°
15°
¾"
2"
4"

U BOTTOM
CUT 2

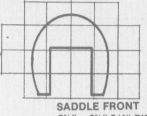

BACK EDGE
SEAT CUT

SADDLE REAR
7½" x 8⅜" x 5/4" PINE

MATERIAL LIST FOR PRANCER

AMOUNT	ITEM
2 pkg. (20)	Brass grommets, size o
1	Brass garment snap
2	1" i.d. ring, brass
2	¾" brass buckle
3-4 SF	6-7 oz. utility leather
20 LF	5/4" x 12" Pine stairtread
10 LF	2" x 12" Pine for rockers

SADDLE FRONT
6⅝" x 6⅜" 5/4" PINE

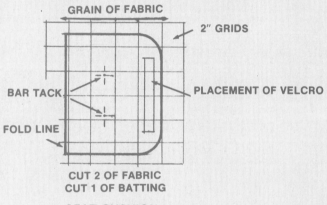

GRAIN OF FABRIC

2" GRIDS

BAR TACK

PLACEMENT OF VELCRO

FOLD LINE

CUT 2 OF FABRIC
CUT 1 OF BATTING

SEAT CUSHION

NOTES:

STUDY THE PLANS CAREFULLY.

SAND SURFACES. NAILS SHOULD BE
SET. PUTTY NAIL HOLES WHEN
FINISHING.

CHECK CATALOG FOR PAINTING SUGGESTIONS.
USE STAIN OF CHOICE, THEN TWO COATS OF
URETHANE GLOSS SPAR VARNISH, SANDING
BETWEEN COATS.

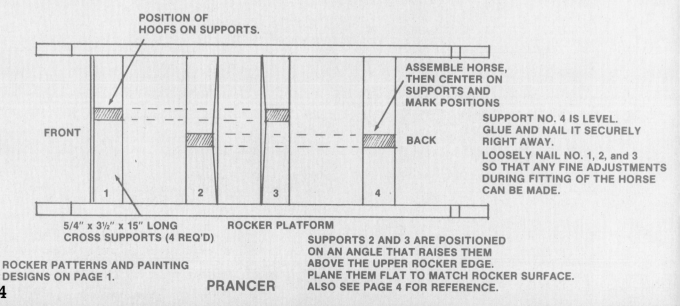

POSITION OF
HOOFS ON SUPPORTS.

ASSEMBLE HORSE,
THEN CENTER ON
SUPPORTS AND
MARK POSITIONS

FRONT

BACK

1   2   3   4

SUPPORT NO. 4 IS LEVEL.
GLUE AND NAIL IT SECURELY
RIGHT AWAY.
LOOSELY NAIL NO. 1, 2, and 3
SO THAT ANY FINE ADJUSTMENTS
DURING FITTING OF THE HORSE
CAN BE MADE.

5/4" x 3½" x 15" LONG
CROSS SUPPORTS (4 REQ'D)

ROCKER PLATFORM

ROCKER PATTERNS AND PAINTING
DESIGNS ON PAGE 1.

PRANCER

SUPPORTS 2 AND 3 ARE POSITIONED
ON AN ANGLE THAT RAISES THEM
ABOVE THE UPPER ROCKER EDGE.
PLANE THEM FLAT TO MATCH ROCKER SURFACE.
ALSO SEE PAGE 4 FOR REFERENCE.

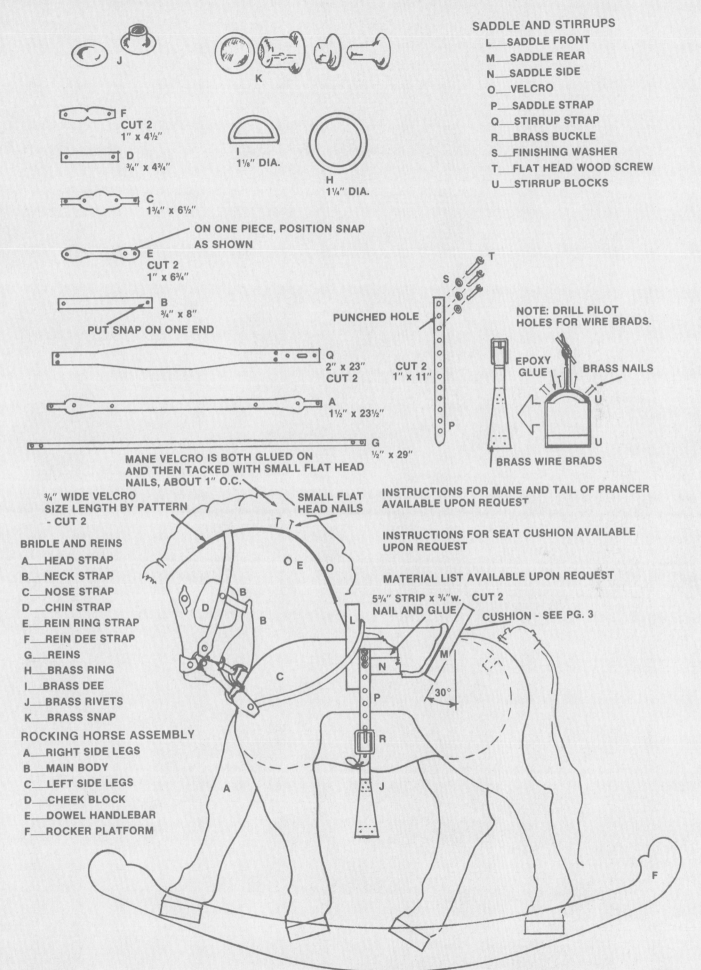

SADDLE AND STIRRUPS

L___SADDLE FRONT
M___SADDLE REAR
N___SADDLE SIDE
O___VELCRO
P___SADDLE STRAP
Q___STIRRUP STRAP
R___BRASS BUCKLE
S___FINISHING WASHER
T___FLAT HEAD WOOD SCREW
U___STIRRUP BLOCKS

J

K

F
CUT 2
1" x 4½"

D
¾" x 4¾"

I
1⅛" DIA.

H
1¼" DIA.

C
1¾" x 6½"

ON ONE PIECE, POSITION SNAP
AS SHOWN

E
CUT 2
1" x 6¾"

B
¾" x 8"
PUT SNAP ON ONE END

PUNCHED HOLE

CUT 2
1" x 11"

P

NOTE: DRILL PILOT
HOLES FOR WIRE BRADS.

EPOXY
GLUE

BRASS NAILS

U

U

BRASS WIRE BRADS

Q
2" x 23"
CUT 2

A
1½" x 23½"

G
½" x 29"

MANE VELCRO IS BOTH GLUED ON
AND THEN TACKED WITH SMALL FLAT HEAD
NAILS, ABOUT 1" O.C.

¾" WIDE VELCRO
SIZE LENGTH BY PATTERN
- CUT 2

SMALL FLAT
HEAD NAILS

INSTRUCTIONS FOR MANE AND TAIL OF PRANCER
AVAILABLE UPON REQUEST

INSTRUCTIONS FOR SEAT CUSHION AVAILABLE
UPON REQUEST

MATERIAL LIST AVAILABLE UPON REQUEST

5¾" STRIP x ¾"w.   CUT 2
NAIL AND GLUE

CUSHION - SEE PG. 3

30°

BRIDLE AND REINS

A___HEAD STRAP
B___NECK STRAP
C___NOSE STRAP
D___CHIN STRAP
E___REIN RING STRAP
F___REIN DEE STRAP
G___REINS
H___BRASS RING
I___BRASS DEE
J___BRASS RIVETS
K___BRASS SNAP

ROCKING HORSE ASSEMBLY

A___RIGHT SIDE LEGS
B___MAIN BODY
C___LEFT SIDE LEGS
D___CHEEK BLOCK
E___DOWEL HANDLEBAR
F___ROCKER PLATFORM

STAKE TRUCK AND TRAILER

This is a favorite. A tough truck and trailer for all those big jobs around the house, completes your truck fleet. Size: Trailer 8″ long, 7″ wide. Truck 19″ long, 7″ wide.

BOOM CRANE

Fully workable boom retracts from 34″ to 19″, and is adjustable from a horizontal position up to about 60°. Color-coded hand cranks and brake knobs for easy co-ordination. Size: 14″ long, 9″ wide.

BOOM CRANE

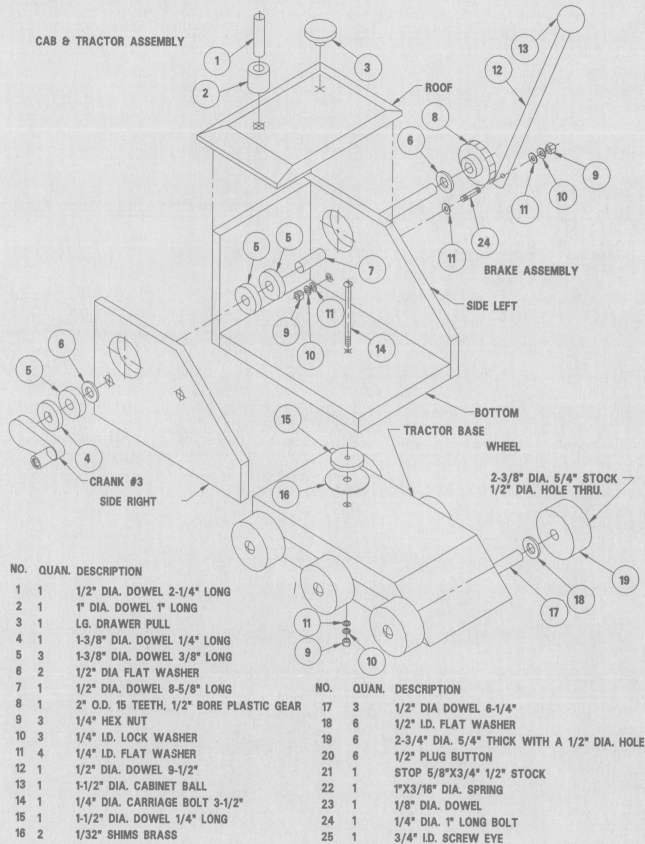

CAB & TRACTOR ASSEMBLY

ROOF

BRAKE ASSEMBLY

SIDE LEFT

BOTTOM

TRACTOR BASE

WHEEL

2-3/8" DIA. 5/4" STOCK
1/2" DIA. HOLE THRU.

CRANK #3

SIDE RIGHT

NO.	QUAN.	DESCRIPTION
1	1	1/2" DIA. DOWEL 2-1/4" LONG
2	1	1" DIA. DOWEL 1" LONG
3	1	LG. DRAWER PULL
4	1	1-3/8" DIA. DOWEL 1/4" LONG
5	3	1-3/8" DIA. DOWEL 3/8" LONG
6	2	1/2" DIA FLAT WASHER
7	1	1/2" DIA. DOWEL 8-5/8" LONG
8	1	2" O.D. 15 TEETH, 1/2" BORE PLASTIC GEAR
9	3	1/4" HEX NUT
10	3	1/4" I.D. LOCK WASHER
11	4	1/4" I.D. FLAT WASHER
12	1	1/2" DIA. DOWEL 9-1/2"
13	1	1-1/2" DIA. CABINET BALL
14	1	1/4" DIA. CARRIAGE BOLT 3-1/2"
15	1	1-1/2" DIA. DOWEL 1/4" LONG
16	2	1/32" SHIMS BRASS

NO.	QUAN.	DESCRIPTION
17	3	1/2" DIA DOWEL 6-1/4"
18	6	1/2" I.D. FLAT WASHER
19	6	2-3/4" DIA. 5/4" THICK WITH A 1/2" DIA. HOLE
20	6	1/2" PLUG BUTTON
21	1	STOP 5/8"X3/4" 1/2" STOCK
22	1	1"X3/16" DIA. SPRING
23	1	1/8" DIA. DOWEL
24	1	1/4" DIA. 1" LONG BOLT
25	1	3/4" I.D. SCREW EYE

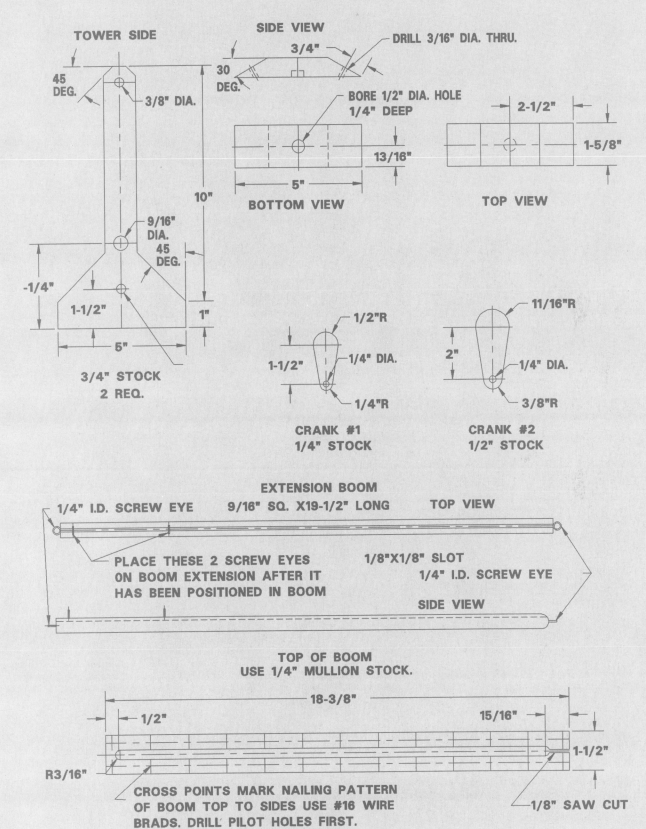

TOWER SIDE

45 DEG.

3/8" DIA.

9/16" DIA.
45 DEG.

-1/4"

1-1/2"

5"

10"

1"

3/4" STOCK
2 REQ.

SIDE VIEW

3/4"

DRILL 3/16" DIA. THRU.

30 DEG.

BORE 1/2" DIA. HOLE
1/4" DEEP

13/16"

5"

BOTTOM VIEW

2-1/2"

1-5/8"

TOP VIEW

1/2"R

1/4" DIA.

1-1/2"

1/4"R

CRANK #1
1/4" STOCK

11/16"R

2"

1/4" DIA.

3/8"R

CRANK #2
1/2" STOCK

EXTENSION BOOM

1/4" I.D. SCREW EYE   9/16" SQ. X19-1/2" LONG   TOP VIEW

PLACE THESE 2 SCREW EYES
ON BOOM EXTENSION AFTER IT
HAS BEEN POSITIONED IN BOOM

1/8"X1/8" SLOT
1/4" I.D. SCREW EYE

SIDE VIEW

TOP OF BOOM
USE 1/4" MULLION STOCK.

18-3/8"

1/2"

15/16"

1-1/2"

R3/16"

1/8" SAW CUT

CROSS POINTS MARK NAILING PATTERN
OF BOOM TOP TO SIDES USE #16 WIRE
BRADS. DRILL PILOT HOLES FIRST.

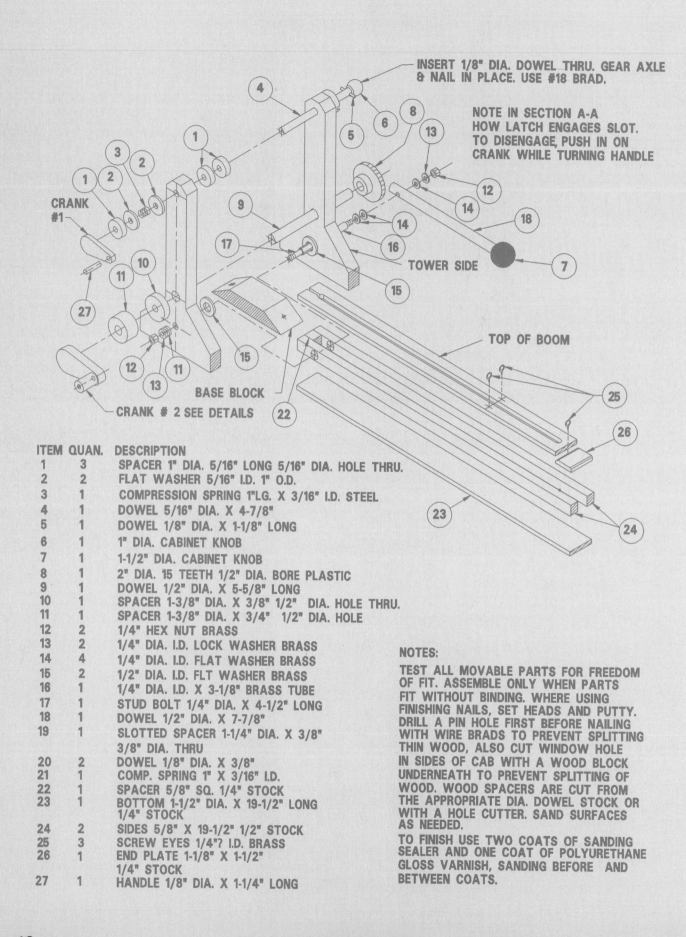

INSERT 1/8" DIA. DOWEL THRU. GEAR AXLE & NAIL IN PLACE. USE #18 BRAD.

NOTE IN SECTION A-A HOW LATCH ENGAGES SLOT. TO DISENGAGE, PUSH IN ON CRANK WHILE TURNING HANDLE

CRANK #1

TOWER SIDE

TOP OF BOOM

BASE BLOCK

CRANK # 2 SEE DETAILS

ITEM	QUAN.	DESCRIPTION
1	3	SPACER 1" DIA. 5/16" LONG 5/16" DIA. HOLE THRU.
2	2	FLAT WASHER 5/16" I.D. 1" O.D.
3	1	COMPRESSION SPRING 1"LG. X 3/16" I.D. STEEL
4	1	DOWEL 5/16" DIA. X 4-7/8"
5	1	DOWEL 1/8" DIA. X 1-1/8" LONG
6	1	1" DIA. CABINET KNOB
7	1	1-1/2" DIA. CABINET KNOB
8	1	2" DIA. 15 TEETH 1/2" DIA. BORE PLASTIC
9	1	DOWEL 1/2" DIA. X 5-5/8" LONG
10	1	SPACER 1-3/8" DIA. X 3/8" 1/2" DIA. HOLE THRU.
11	1	SPACER 1-3/8" DIA. X 3/4" 1/2" DIA. HOLE
12	2	1/4" HEX NUT BRASS
13	2	1/4" DIA. I.D. LOCK WASHER BRASS
14	4	1/4" DIA. I.D. FLAT WASHER BRASS
15	2	1/2" DIA. I.D. FLT WASHER BRASS
16	1	1/4" DIA. I.D. X 3-1/8" BRASS TUBE
17	1	STUD BOLT 1/4" DIA. X 4-1/2" LONG
18	1	DOWEL 1/2" DIA. X 7-7/8"
19	1	SLOTTED SPACER 1-1/4" DIA. X 3/8" 3/8" DIA. THRU
20	2	DOWEL 1/8" DIA. X 3/8"
21	1	COMP. SPRING 1" X 3/16" I.D.
22	1	SPACER 5/8" SQ. 1/4" STOCK
23	1	BOTTOM 1-1/2" DIA. X 19-1/2" LONG 1/4" STOCK
24	2	SIDES 5/8" X 19-1/2" 1/2" STOCK
25	3	SCREW EYES 1/4"? I.D. BRASS
26	1	END PLATE 1-1/8" X 1-1/2" 1/4" STOCK
27	1	HANDLE 1/8" DIA. X 1-1/4" LONG

NOTES:

TEST ALL MOVABLE PARTS FOR FREEDOM OF FIT. ASSEMBLE ONLY WHEN PARTS FIT WITHOUT BINDING. WHERE USING FINISHING NAILS, SET HEADS AND PUTTY. DRILL A PIN HOLE FIRST BEFORE NAILING WITH WIRE BRADS TO PREVENT SPLITTING THIN WOOD, ALSO CUT WINDOW HOLE IN SIDES OF CAB WITH A WOOD BLOCK UNDERNEATH TO PREVENT SPLITTING OF WOOD. WOOD SPACERS ARE CUT FROM THE APPROPRIATE DIA. DOWEL STOCK OR WITH A HOLE CUTTER. SAND SURFACES AS NEEDED.

TO FINISH USE TWO COATS OF SANDING SEALER AND ONE COAT OF POLYURETHANE GLOSS VARNISH, SANDING BEFORE AND BETWEEN COATS.

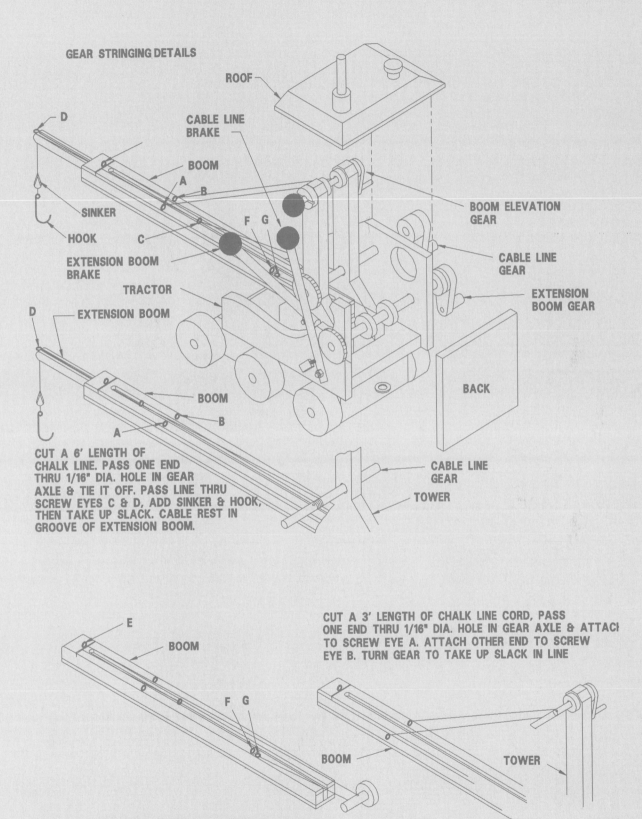

GEAR STRINGING DETAILS

ROOF

CABLE LINE
BRAKE

D

BOOM

A

B

CABLE LINE BRAKE

SINKER

BOOM ELEVATION
GEAR

HOOK

C

F G

CABLE LINE
GEAR

EXTENSION BOOM
BRAKE

TRACTOR

EXTENSION
BOOM GEAR

D

EXTENSION BOOM

BOOM

BACK

B

A

CABLE LINE
GEAR

CUT A 6' LENGTH OF
CHALK LINE. PASS ONE END
THRU 1/16" DIA. HOLE IN GEAR
AXLE & TIE IT OFF. PASS LINE THRU
SCREW EYES C & D, ADD SINKER & HOOK,
THEN TAKE UP SLACK. CABLE REST IN
GROOVE OF EXTENSION BOOM.

TOWER

E

BOOM

CUT A 3' LENGTH OF CHALK LINE CORD, PASS
ONE END THRU 1/16" DIA. HOLE IN GEAR AXLE & ATTACH
TO SCREW EYE A. ATTACH OTHER END TO SCREW
EYE B. TURN GEAR TO TAKE UP SLACK IN LINE

F G

BOOM

TOWER

CUT A 4' LENGTH OF CHALK LINE. PASS ONE END
THRU 1/16" DIA. HOLE IN GEAR AXLE AND ATTACH TO
SCREW EYE G. WRAP OTHER END IN REVERSE
DIRECTION AROUND AXLE AND PASS THRU SCREW EYE E,
THEN TIE OFF AT SCREW EYE F, TAKE UP SLACK.

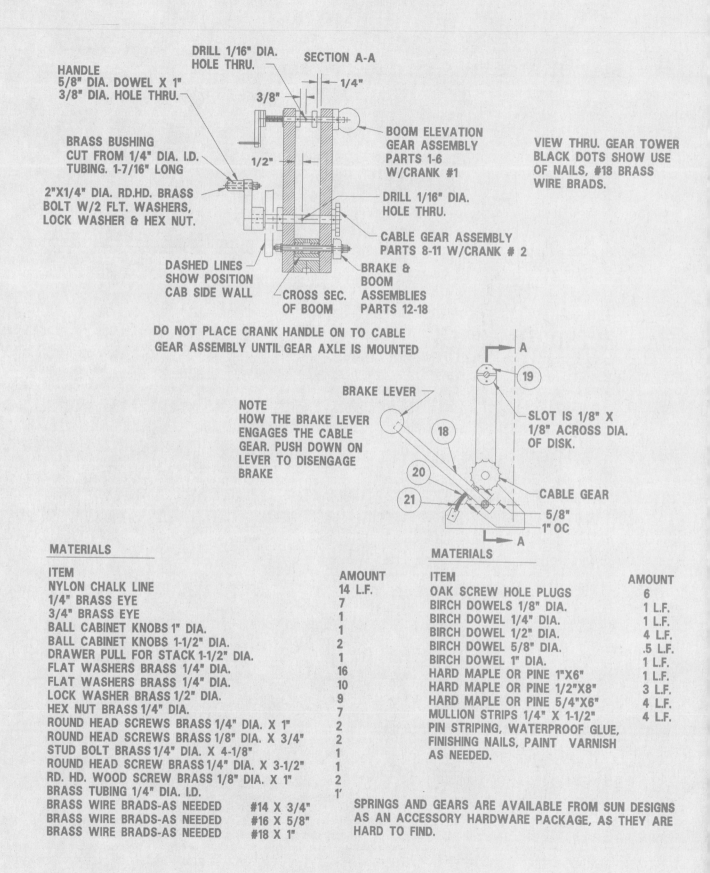

HANDLE
5/8" DIA. DOWEL X 1"
3/8" DIA. HOLE THRU.

DRILL 1/16" DIA.
HOLE THRU.

SECTION A-A

BRASS BUSHING
CUT FROM 1/4" DIA. I.D.
TUBING. 1-7/16" LONG

2"X1/4" DIA. RD.HD. BRASS
BOLT W/2 FLT. WASHERS,
LOCK WASHER & HEX NUT.

BOOM ELEVATION
GEAR ASSEMBLY
PARTS 1-6
W/CRANK #1

VIEW THRU. GEAR TOWER
BLACK DOTS SHOW USE
OF NAILS, #18 BRASS
WIRE BRADS.

DRILL 1/16" DIA.
HOLE THRU.

CABLE GEAR ASSEMBLY
PARTS 8-11 W/CRANK # 2

DASHED LINES
SHOW POSITION
CAB SIDE WALL

CROSS SEC.
OF BOOM

BRAKE &
BOOM
ASSEMBLIES
PARTS 12-18

DO NOT PLACE CRANK HANDLE ON TO CABLE
GEAR ASSEMBLY UNTIL GEAR AXLE IS MOUNTED

BRAKE LEVER

NOTE
HOW THE BRAKE LEVER
ENGAGES THE CABLE
GEAR. PUSH DOWN ON
LEVER TO DISENGAGE
BRAKE

SLOT IS 1/8" X
1/8" ACROSS DIA.
OF DISK.

CABLE GEAR

5/8"
1" OC

MATERIALS

ITEM	AMOUNT
NYLON CHALK LINE	14 L.F.
1/4" BRASS EYE	7
3/4" BRASS EYE	1
BALL CABINET KNOBS 1" DIA.	1
BALL CABINET KNOBS 1-1/2" DIA.	2
DRAWER PULL FOR STACK 1-1/2" DIA.	1
FLAT WASHERS BRASS 1/4" DIA.	16
FLAT WASHERS BRASS 1/4" DIA.	10
LOCK WASHER BRASS 1/2" DIA.	9
HEX NUT BRASS 1/4" DIA.	7
ROUND HEAD SCREWS BRASS 1/4" DIA. X 1"	2
ROUND HEAD SCREWS BRASS 1/8" DIA. X 3/4"	2
STUD BOLT BRASS 1/4" DIA. X 4-1/8"	1
ROUND HEAD SCREW BRASS 1/4" DIA. X 3-1/2"	1
RD. HD. WOOD SCREW BRASS 1/8" DIA. X 1"	2
BRASS TUBING 1/4" DIA. I.D.	1'
BRASS WIRE BRADS-AS NEEDED #14 X 3/4"	
BRASS WIRE BRADS-AS NEEDED #16 X 5/8"	
BRASS WIRE BRADS-AS NEEDED #18 X 1"	

MATERIALS

ITEM	AMOUNT
OAK SCREW HOLE PLUGS	6
BIRCH DOWELS 1/8" DIA.	1 L.F.
BIRCH DOWEL 1/4" DIA.	1 L.F.
BIRCH DOWEL 1/2" DIA.	4 L.F.
BIRCH DOWEL 5/8" DIA.	.5 L.F.
BIRCH DOWEL 1" DIA.	1 L.F.
HARD MAPLE OR PINE 1"X6"	1 L.F.
HARD MAPLE OR PINE 1/2"X8"	3 L.F.
HARD MAPLE OR PINE 5/4"X6"	4 L.F.
MULLION STRIPS 1/4" X 1-1/2"	4 L.F.

PIN STRIPING, WATERPROOF GLUE,
FINISHING NAILS, PAINT VARNISH
AS NEEDED.

SPRINGS AND GEARS ARE AVAILABLE FROM SUN DESIGNS
AS AN ACCESSORY HARDWARE PACKAGE, AS THEY ARE
HARD TO FIND.

STAKE TRUCK & TRAILER

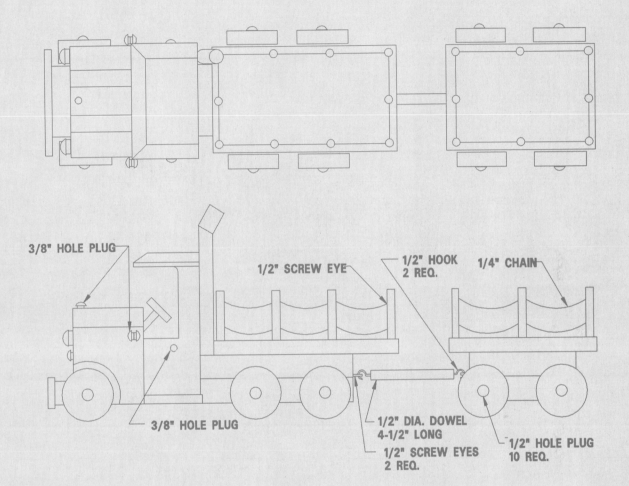

3/8" HOLE PLUG

3/8" HOLE PLUG

1/2" SCREW EYE

1/2" HOOK
2 REQ.

1/4" CHAIN

1/2" DIA. DOWEL
4-1/2" LONG

1/2" SCREW EYES
2 REQ.

1/2" HOLE PLUG
10 REQ.

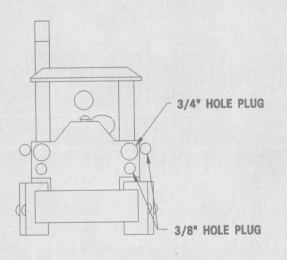

3/4" HOLE PLUG

3/8" HOLE PLUG

GENERAL NOTES:

READ AND STUDY PLANS CAREFULLY
BEFORE BEGINNING PROJECT.

TEST ALL MOVABLE PARTS FOR
FREEDOM OF FIT, ASSEMBLE ONLY
WHEN PARTS FIT WITHOUT BINDING

SAND SURFACES, SET ALL FINISHING
NAILS AND PUTTY NAIL HOLES WHEN
FINISHING.

TO FINISH USE TWO COATS OF SEALER
AND ONE COAT OF SPAR VARNISH,
SANDING BETWEEN COATS.

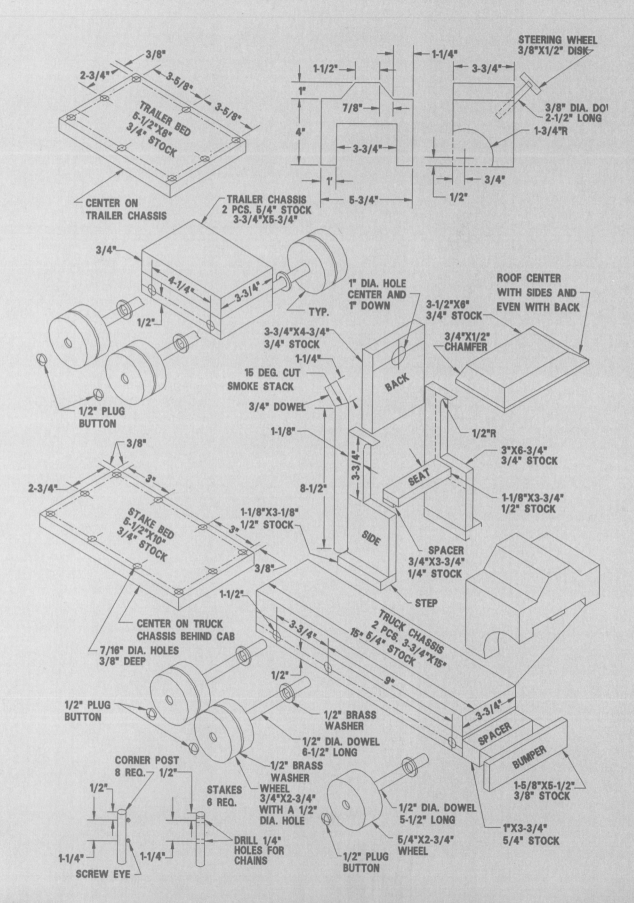

STEERING WHEEL
3/8"X1/2" DISK

3/8" DIA. DO[...]
2-1/2" LONG

1-3/4"R

3/8"
2-3/4"
3-5/8"
3-5/8"

TRAILER BED
5-1/2"X8"
3/4" STOCK

1-1/4"
1-1/2"
1"
7/8"
4"
3-3/4"
5-3/4"
1"
1/2"
3-3/4"
3/4"

CENTER ON
TRAILER CHASSIS

TRAILER CHASSIS
2 PCS. 5/4" STOCK
3-3/4"X5-3/4"

3/4"
4-1/4"
3-3/4"
1/2"

TYP.

1" DIA. HOLE
CENTER AND
1" DOWN

ROOF CENTER
WITH SIDES AND
EVEN WITH BACK

3-1/2"X6"
3/4" STOCK

BACK

3/4"X1/2"
CHAMFER

1/2"R

3-3/4"X4-3/4"
3/4" STOCK

1-1/4"

15 DEG. CUT
SMOKE STACK

3/4" DOWEL

1-1/8"

3-3/4"

8-1/2"

SEAT

3"X6-3/4"
3/4" STOCK

1-1/8"X3-3/4"
1/2" STOCK

1/2" PLUG
BUTTON

3/8"
2-3/4"
3"

STAKE BED
5-1/2"X10"
3/4" STOCK

3"
1-1/8"X3-1/8"
1/2" STOCK

3/8"

SIDE

SPACER
3/4"X3-3/4"
1/4" STOCK

STEP

CENTER ON TRUCK
CHASSIS BEHIND CAB

7/16" DIA. HOLES
3/8" DEEP

TRUCK CHASSIS
2 PCS. 3-3/4"X15"
15" 5/4" STOCK

3-3/4"
1/2"
9"

3-3/4"

SPACER

1/2" PLUG
BUTTON

1/2" BRASS
WASHER

1/2" DIA. DOWEL
6-1/2" LONG

1/2" BRASS
WASHER
WHEEL
3/4"X2-3/4"
WITH A 1/2"
DIA. HOLE

BUMPER

1-5/8"X5-1/2"
3/8" STOCK

1"X3-3/4"
5/4" STOCK

CORNER POST
8 REQ.

1/2"
1/2"

STAKES
6 REQ.

DRILL 1/4"
HOLES FOR
CHAINS

1/2" DIA. DOWEL
5-1/2" LONG

5/4"X2-3/4"
WHEEL

1/2" PLUG
BUTTON

1/2"

1-1/4"
1-1/4"

SCREW EYE

44

CONVERTIBLE STAKE WAGON

The ultimate in elegance for work or play, summer and winter, complete with opera windows and a continental wheel. The wood-rail sides are quickly put on and can be removed in seconds by simply lifting them up from the interlocking wood corners. There are even optional runners for winter. Size: 37½" long, 19" wide, 21½" high without canopy.

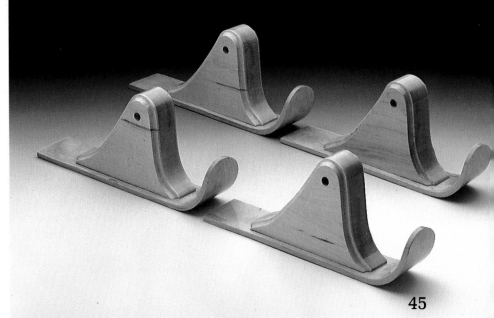

45

CONVERTIBLE STAKE WAGON

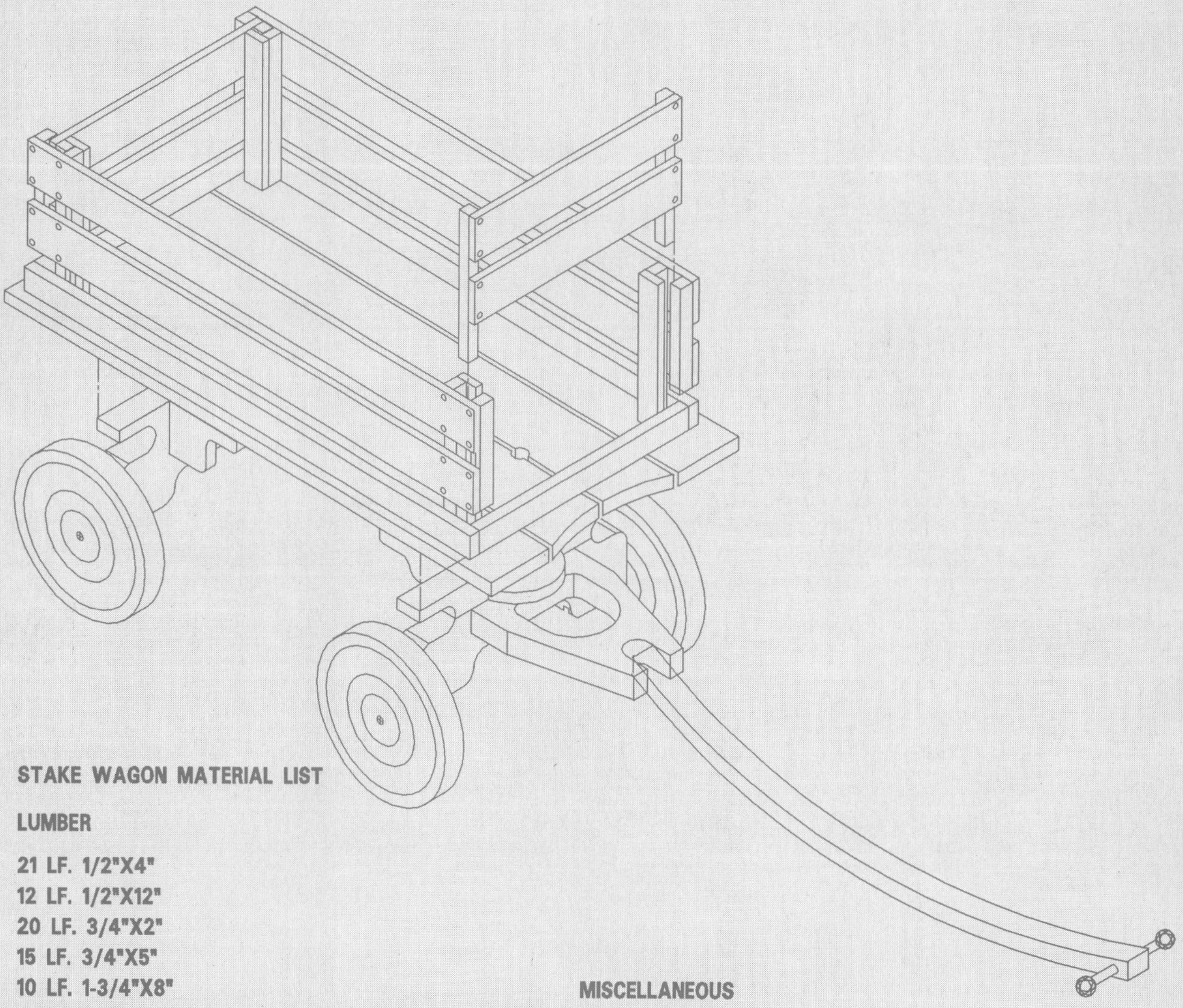

STAKE WAGON MATERIAL LIST

LUMBER

21 LF. 1/2"X4"
12 LF. 1/2"X12"
20 LF. 3/4"X2"
15 LF. 3/4"X5"
10 LF. 1-3/4"X8"
4 LF. 1"X10"
16 SF. 1/16" VENEER

HARDWARE

1 HEX. HD. BOLT 1/4" DIA. X4-3/8"
1 STOVE BOLT 1/4" DIA. X 4-1/2"
74 1" NO. 8 FLT HD. WOOD SCREW
20 1-1/2" NO. 8 FLT. HD. WOOD SCREW
2 2-1/2" NO. 8 FLT. HD. WOOD SCREW
6 1-1/2" NO. 10 FLT. HD. WOOD SCREW
8 3" NO. 10 FLT. HD. WOOD SCREW
4 3/8" DIA. X 20" AXLES
8 LOCKING HUB NUTS
16 3/8" I.D. FLAT WASHERS
4 1/2"X1-1/2" METAL STRIPS

MISCELLANEOUS

6 LF. NEOPRENE RUBBER 1"X1/8"
1 LF. 1/2" DIA. DOWEL

RECOMMENDED WOOD HARD MAPLE OR OAK
AS DESIRED, WAX FOR SKI RUNNERS.GLUE,
STAIN, PAINT, OR POLYURETHANE FINISH.
ALLOW 10% CONSTRUCTION WASTE .
USE BRASS HARDWARE WHERE POSSIBLE.
AXLES, SKIS, BENTWOOD HANDLE, RED METAL
WHEELS, HARDWARE, WHEEL COVERS AND
CANOPY TOP AVAILABLE FROM SUN DESIGNS.

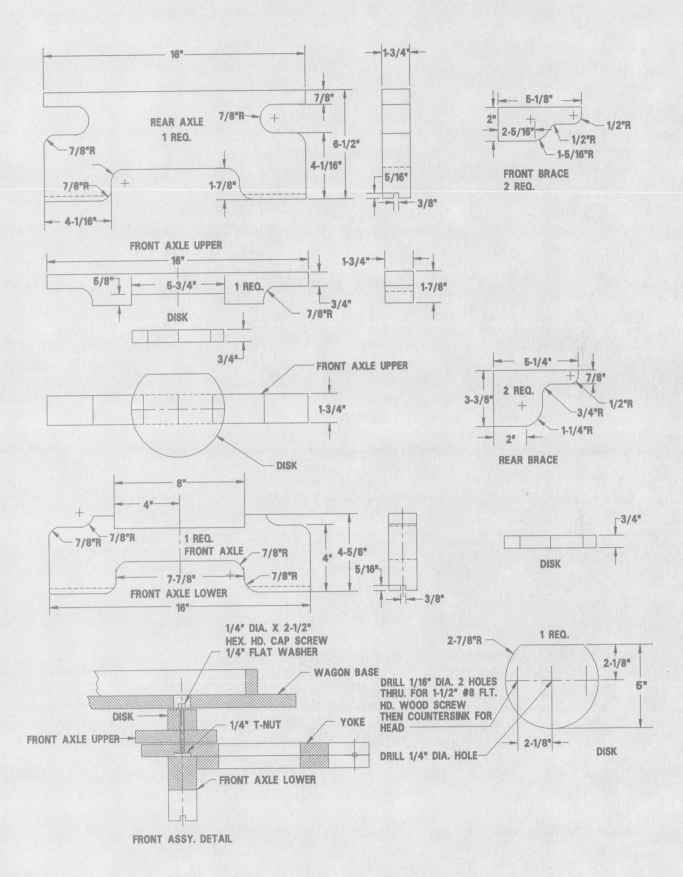

REAR AXLE
1 REQ.

FRONT AXLE UPPER
1 REQ.

DISK

FRONT AXLE UPPER

DISK

FRONT BRACE
2 REQ.

REAR BRACE
2 REQ.

DISK

1 REQ.
FRONT AXLE
FRONT AXLE LOWER

1/4" DIA. X 2-1/2"
HEX. HD. CAP SCREW
1/4" FLAT WASHER
WAGON BASE
DISK
FRONT AXLE UPPER
1/4" T-NUT
YOKE
FRONT AXLE LOWER

FRONT ASSY. DETAIL

DRILL 1/16" DIA. 2 HOLES
THRU. FOR 1-1/2" #8 FLT.
HD. WOOD SCREW
THEN COUNTERSINK FOR
HEAD

DRILL 1/4" DIA. HOLE

1 REQ.
DISK

47

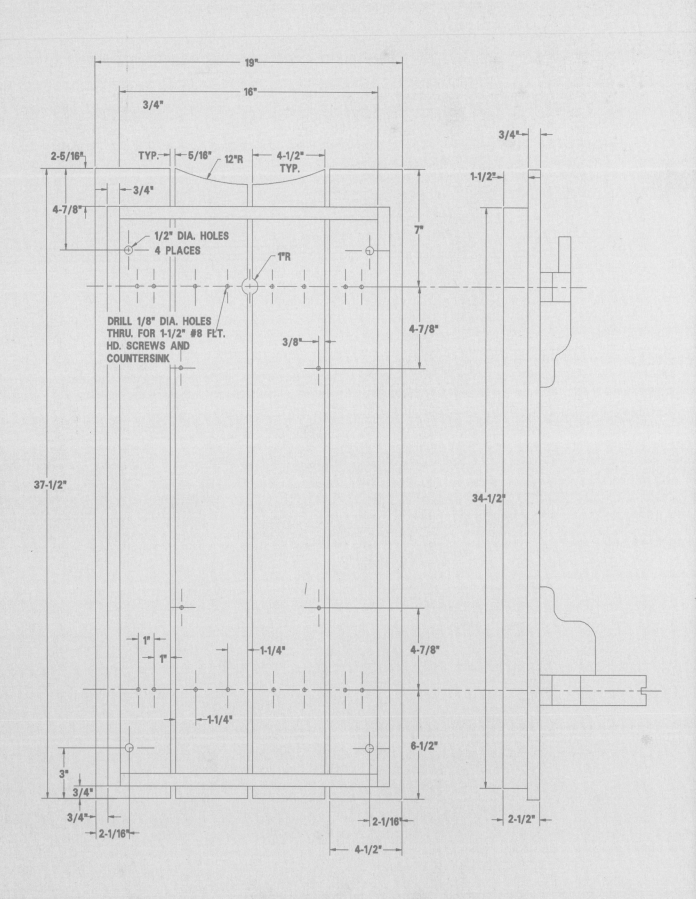

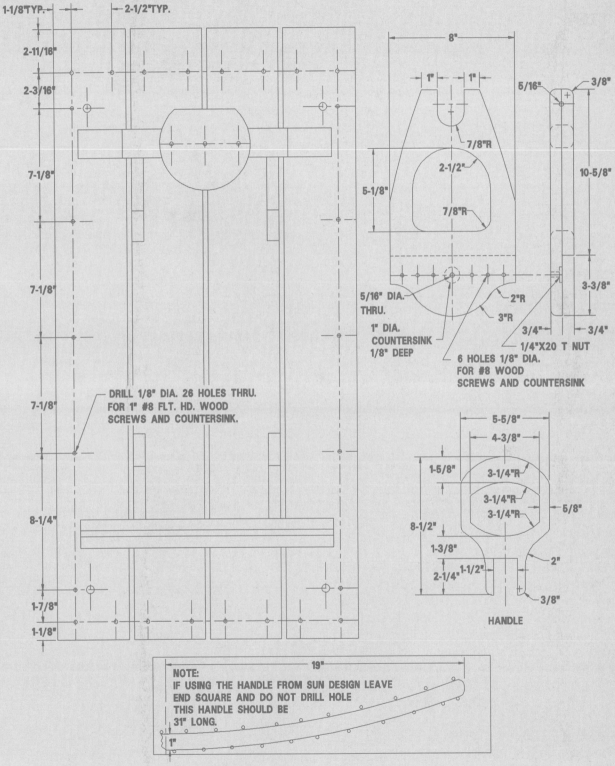

1-1/8"TYP.
2-1/2"TYP.
2-11/16"
2-3/16"
7-1/8"
7-1/8"
7-1/8"
8-1/4"
1-7/8"
1-1/8"

DRILL 1/8" DIA. 26 HOLES THRU.
FOR 1" #8 FLT. HD. WOOD
SCREWS AND COUNTERSINK.

8"
1" 1"
5/16" 3/8"
7/8"R
2-1/2"
5-1/8"
7/8"R
10-5/8"
3-3/8"
5/16" DIA.
THRU.
1" DIA.
COUNTERSINK
1/8" DEEP
2"R
3"R
3/4" 3/4"
1/4"X20 T NUT
6 HOLES 1/8" DIA.
FOR #8 WOOD
SCREWS AND COUNTERSINK

5-5/8"
4-3/8"
1-5/8"
3-1/4"R
3-1/4"R
5/8"
3-1/4"R
8-1/2"
1-3/8"
2"
2-1/4" 1-1/2"
3/8"

HANDLE

19"
NOTE:
IF USING THE HANDLE FROM SUN DESIGN LEAVE
END SQUARE AND DO NOT DRILL HOLE
THIS HANDLE SHOULD BE
31" LONG.
1"

NOTE:
USE 3/4" STOCK (1"X6") 42" LONG TO TRACE PATTERN ON. TRACE PATTERN, TURN OVER, MATCH UP CENTER
LINE AND TRACE OTHER HALF OF PATTERN
CUT 3/16" THICK STRIPS (5 REQ.) FROM 1-1/2" STOCK APROX. 36" LONG. SOAK IN HOT WATER THEN BEND TOGETHER
AS SHOWN IN NAIL OUTLINE. LEAVE 48 HRS. WHEN DRY, GLUE AND CLAMP STRIPS, CUT TO FINISHED SIZE, DRILL,
SAND EDGES ROUND.

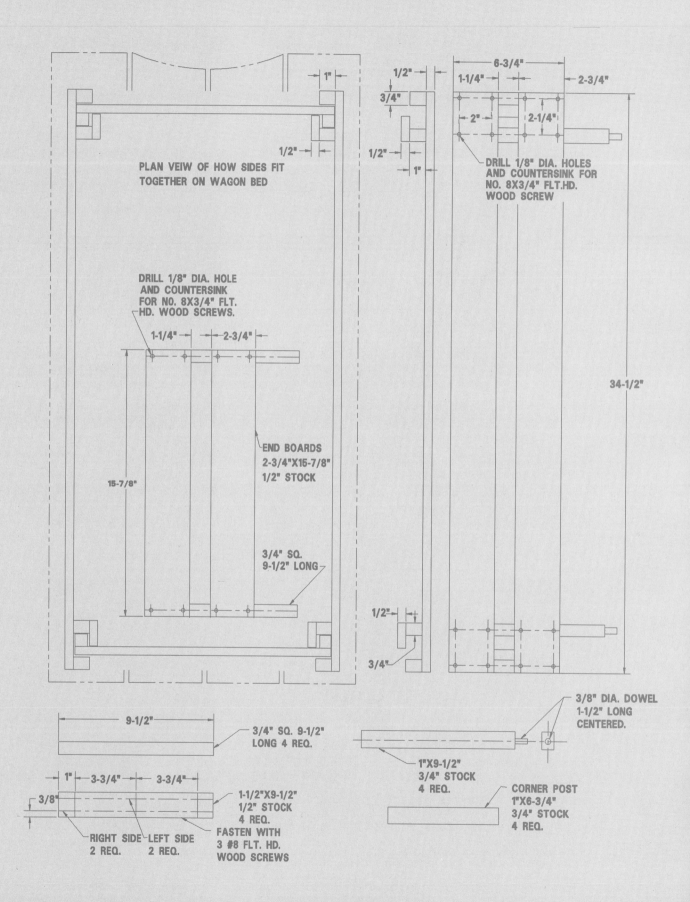

PLAN VEIW OF HOW SIDES FIT TOGETHER ON WAGON BED

1"

1/2"

1/2"

3/4"

1/2"

1"

6-3/4"

1-1/4"

2-3/4"

2"

2-1/4"

DRILL 1/8" DIA. HOLES AND COUNTERSINK FOR NO. 8X3/4" FLT.HD. WOOD SCREW

DRILL 1/8" DIA. HOLE AND COUNTERSINK FOR NO. 8X3/4" FLT. HD. WOOD SCREWS.

1-1/4"

2-3/4"

END BOARDS 2-3/4"X15-7/8" 1/2" STOCK

3/4" SQ. 9-1/2" LONG

15-7/8"

34-1/2"

1/2"

3/4"

3/8" DIA. DOWEL 1-1/2" LONG CENTERED.

9-1/2"

3/4" SQ. 9-1/2" LONG 4 REQ.

1"

3-3/4"

3-3/4"

3/8"

1-1/2"X9-1/2" 1/2" STOCK 4 REQ. FASTEN WITH 3 #8 FLT. HD. WOOD SCREWS

RIGHT SIDE 2 REQ.

LEFT SIDE 2 REQ.

1"X9-1/2" 3/4" STOCK 4 REQ.

CORNER POST 1"X6-3/4" 3/4" STOCK 4 REQ.

50

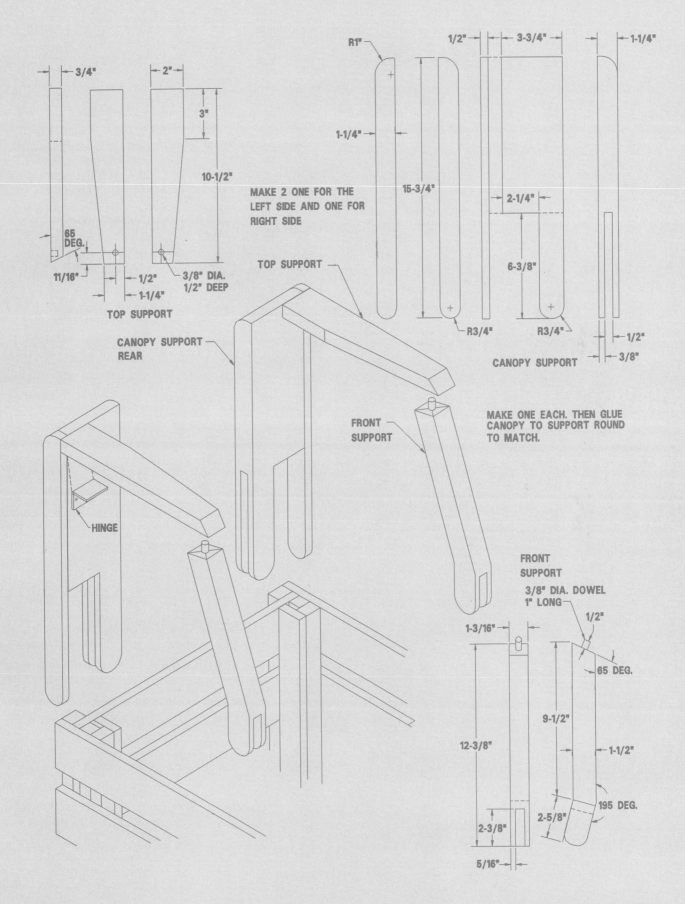

3/4"

2"

3"

10-1/2"

65 DEG.

11/16"

1/2"

1-1/4"

3/8" DIA. 1/2" DEEP

TOP SUPPORT

R1"

1/2"

3-3/4"

1-1/4"

1-1/4"

15-3/4"

2-1/4"

6-3/8"

R3/4"

R3/4"

1/2"

3/8"

MAKE 2 ONE FOR THE LEFT SIDE AND ONE FOR RIGHT SIDE

CANOPY SUPPORT

TOP SUPPORT

CANOPY SUPPORT REAR

FRONT SUPPORT

HINGE

MAKE ONE EACH. THEN GLUE CANOPY TO SUPPORT ROUND TO MATCH.

FRONT SUPPORT

3/8" DIA. DOWEL 1" LONG

1/2"

65 DEG.

1-3/16"

9-1/2"

1-1/2"

12-3/8"

195 DEG.

2-5/8"

2-3/8"

5/16"

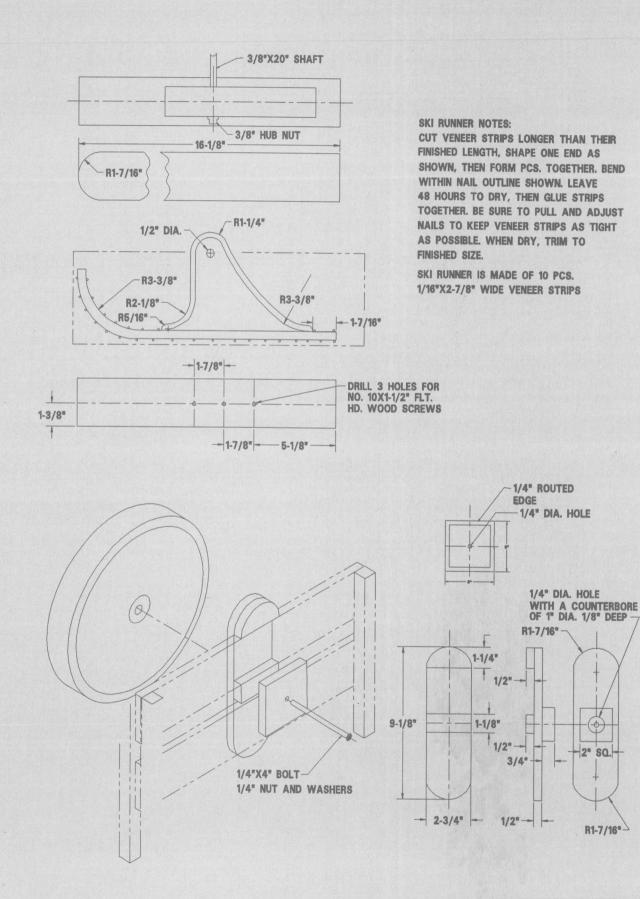

3/8"X20" SHAFT

3/8" HUB NUT

16-1/8"

R1-7/16"

1/2" DIA.

R1-1/4"

R3-3/8"

R2-1/8"

R5/16"

R3-3/8"

1-7/16"

1-7/8"

DRILL 3 HOLES FOR
NO. 10X1-1/2" FLT.
HD. WOOD SCREWS

1-3/8"

1-7/8"

5-1/8"

SKI RUNNER NOTES:
CUT VENEER STRIPS LONGER THAN THEIR
FINISHED LENGTH, SHAPE ONE END AS
SHOWN, THEN FORM PCS. TOGETHER. BEND
WITHIN NAIL OUTLINE SHOWN. LEAVE
48 HOURS TO DRY, THEN GLUE STRIPS
TOGETHER. BE SURE TO PULL AND ADJUST
NAILS TO KEEP VENEER STRIPS AS TIGHT
AS POSSIBLE. WHEN DRY, TRIM TO
FINISHED SIZE.

SKI RUNNER IS MADE OF 10 PCS.
1/16"X2-7/8" WIDE VENEER STRIPS

1/4" ROUTED
EDGE

1/4" DIA. HOLE

1/4" DIA. HOLE
WITH A COUNTERBORE
OF 1" DIA. 1/8" DEEP

R1-7/16"

1-1/4"

1/2"

9-1/8"

1-1/8"

1/2"

3/4"

2" SQ.

2-3/4"

1/2"

R1-7/16"

1/4"X4" BOLT
1/4" NUT AND WASHERS

WHEEL NOTES:

BE SURE TO DRILL THE AXLE HOLE STRAIGHT, OTHER WISE THE WHEEL WILL NOT ROTATE PROPERLY

CUT NEOPRENE TREAD TO EXACT LENGTH. WHEN GLUING, STRETCH IT AROUND THE WHEEL TO A 3/16" OVERLAP, BEND AND BUTT ENDS TOGETHER, PRESS DOWN TIGHT.

APPLY CONTACT CEMENT TO BOTH RUBBER (INCLUDING THE ENDS) AND WOOD, ALLOW TO DRY, THEN APPLY ANOTHER COAT TO BOTH SURFACES, ALLOW THAT TO DRY AS WELL, THEN BOND THE SURFACES TOGETHER.

TURN CONTOUR OF WHEELS AS SHOWN FROM ROUGH CUT WHEEL BLOCKS.

WHEEL BLOCKS ARE BUILT UP FROM 3 PCS. OF 11-3/4" SQ.X1/2" STOCK LAMINATED TOGETHER. BE SURE TO CROSS LAP THE WOOD GRAIN TO PREVENT WARPING.

DRILL A 1/16" DIA. HOLE THRU THE CENTER OF LAMINATED BLOCK TO AID IN DRILLING THE BUSHING HOLE AFTER THE WHEEL IS TURNED

BUSHING AND THE RUBBER TREAD WILL PROTECT AGAINST EXCESSIVE WEAR.

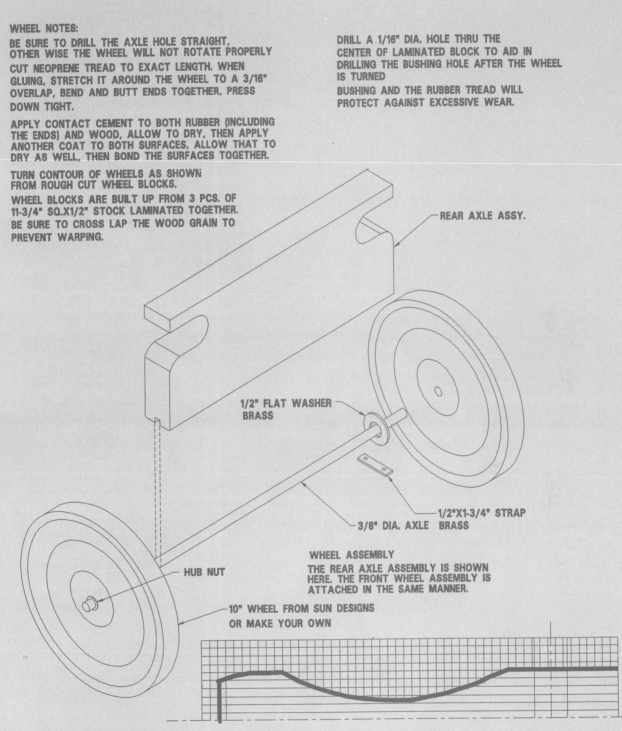

REAR AXLE ASSY.

1/2" FLAT WASHER BRASS

1/2"X1-3/4" STRAP BRASS

3/8" DIA. AXLE

HUB NUT

WHEEL ASSEMBLY

THE REAR AXLE ASSEMBLY IS SHOWN HERE. THE FRONT WHEEL ASSEMBLY IS ATTACHED IN THE SAME MANNER.

10" WHEEL FROM SUN DESIGNS OR MAKE YOUR OWN

EACH SQ. 1/8"

STEAMROLLER
Old-fashioned steamroller and water wagon. Brass drive chain on wheel drives fly-wheel and wood piston back and forth. Steering wheel turns front roller. Size: 15″ long, 10″ high. Water wagon 10″ long.

BULLDOZER
Has an easy-working, up-and-down blade action which is controlled by the handle with the yellow ball. Simulated joy sticks for steering, and instrument panel. Size: 13″ long, 8″ high.

STEAMROLLER

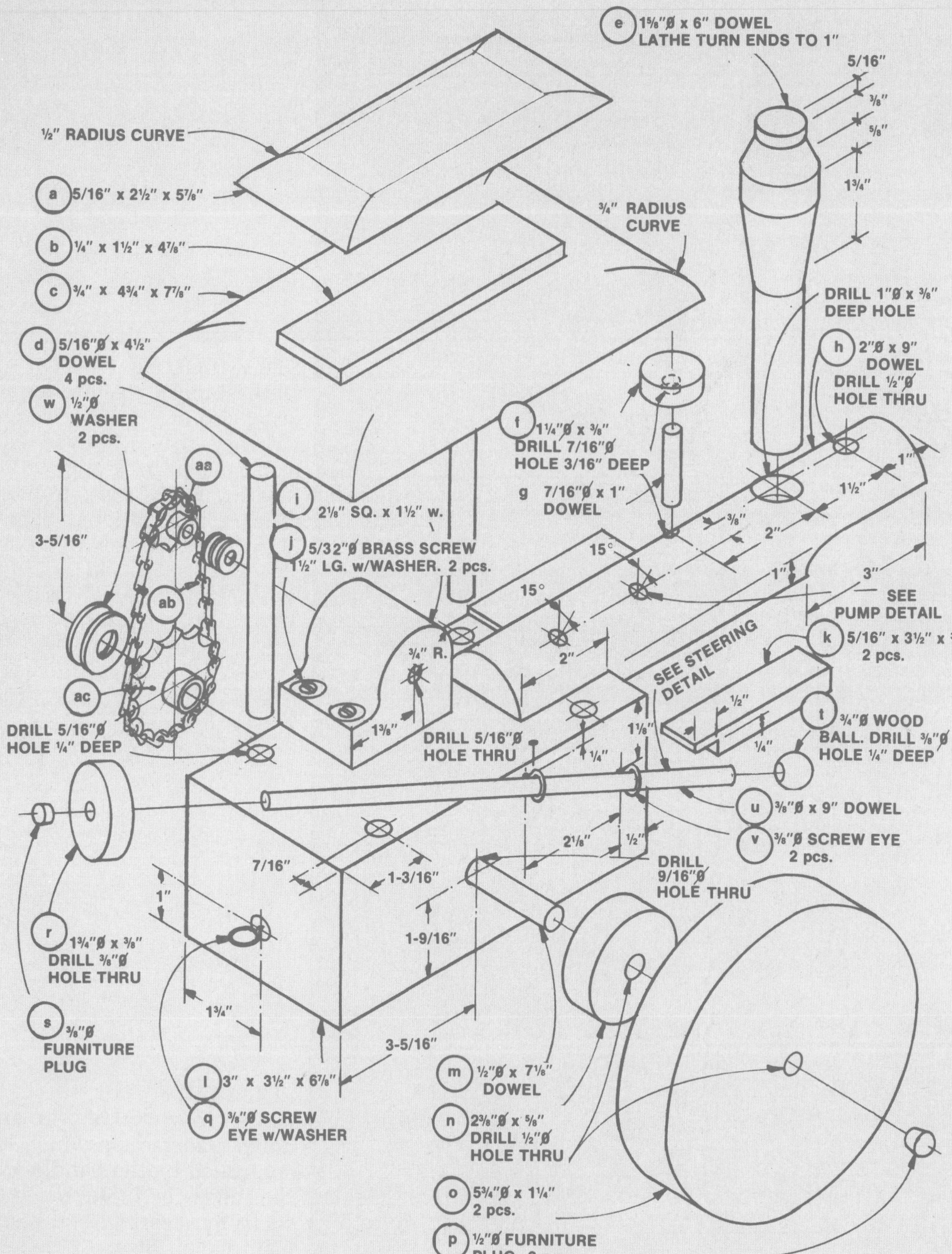

e 1⅝"Ø x 6" DOWEL LATHE TURN ENDS TO 1"
5/16"
⅜"
⅝"
1¾"
½" RADIUS CURVE
a 5/16" x 2½" x 5⅞"
b ¼" x 1½" x 4⅞"
c ¾" x 4¾" x 7⅞"
¾" RADIUS CURVE
DRILL 1"Ø x ⅜" DEEP HOLE
d 5/16"Ø x 4½" DOWEL 4 pcs.
w ½"Ø WASHER 2 pcs.
h 2"Ø x 9" DOWEL DRILL ½"Ø HOLE THRU
f 1¼"Ø x ⅜" DRILL 7/16"Ø HOLE 3/16" DEEP
g 7/16"Ø x 1" DOWEL
aa
i 2⅛" SQ. x 1½" w.
1"
1½"
3-5/16"
j 5/32"Ø BRASS SCREW 1½" LG. w/WASHER. 2 pcs.
⅜"
2"
15°
1"
3"
15°
SEE PUMP DETAIL
ab
¾" R.
k 5/16" x 3½" x ¾" 2 pcs.
2"
SEE STEERING DETAIL
ac
½"
t ¾"Ø WOOD BALL. DRILL ⅜"Ø HOLE ¼" DEEP
DRILL 5/16"Ø HOLE ¼" DEEP
1⅜"
DRILL 5/16"Ø HOLE THRU
1⅛"
¼"
¼"
u ⅜"Ø x 9" DOWEL
v ⅜"Ø SCREW EYE 2 pcs.
2⅛"
½"
7/16"
1-3/16"
DRILL 9/16"Ø HOLE THRU
1"
r 1¾"Ø x ⅜" DRILL ⅜"Ø HOLE THRU
1-9/16"
1¾"
s ⅜"Ø FURNITURE PLUG
3-5/16"
l 3" x 3½" x 6⅞"
m ½"Ø x 7⅛" DOWEL
q ⅜"Ø SCREW EYE w/WASHER
n 2⅜"Ø x ⅝" DRILL ½"Ø HOLE THRU
o 5¾"Ø x 1¼" 2 pcs.
p ½"Ø FURNITURE PLUG. 2 pcs.

NOTES:

THE PLAN NOTED PIECES "a" THRU "bh" SERVE AS YOUR MATERIALS LIST.

PURCHASE SHOULD BE MADE TO ALLOW FOR WASTE.

PAINT AND STAIN AS YOU DESIRE OR AS PICTURED. APPLY SPAR VARNISH COAT OVERALL.

SCALE: 3/8" = 1"

PURCHASE CHAIN AND GEARS FROM SUN DESIGNS OR HARDWARE STORE

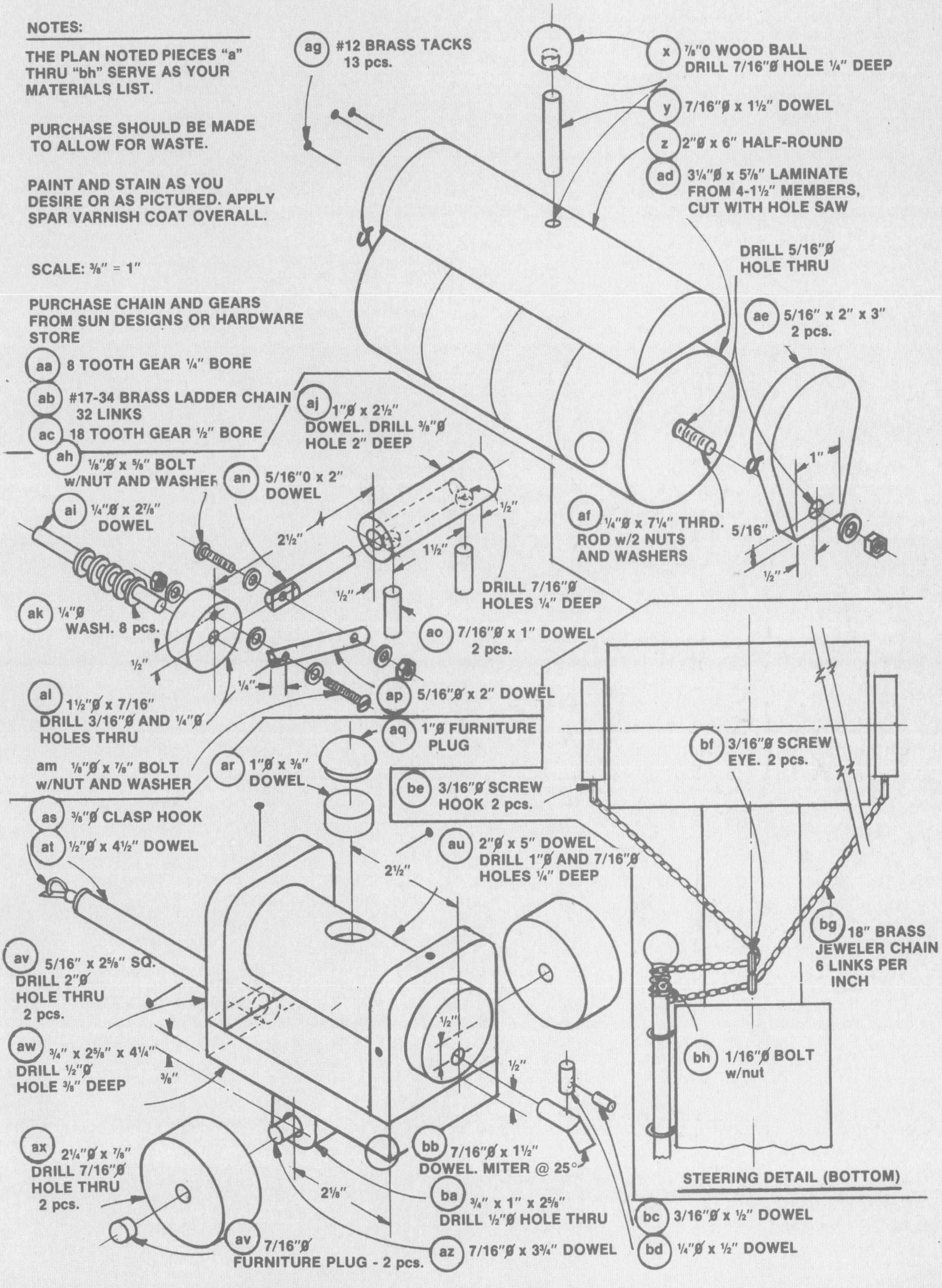
aa 8 TOOTH GEAR 1/4" BORE
ab #17-34 BRASS LADDER CHAIN 32 LINKS
ac 18 TOOTH GEAR 1/2" BORE
ag #12 BRASS TACKS 13 pcs.
x 7/8"0 WOOD BALL DRILL 7/16"Ø HOLE 1/4" DEEP
y 7/16"Ø x 1 1/2" DOWEL
z 2"Ø x 6" HALF-ROUND
ad 3 1/4"Ø x 5 7/8" LAMINATE FROM 4-1 1/2" MEMBERS, CUT WITH HOLE SAW
DRILL 5/16"Ø HOLE THRU
ae 5/16" x 2" x 3" 2 pcs.
aj 1"Ø x 2 1/2" DOWEL. DRILL 3/8"Ø HOLE 2" DEEP
ah 1/8"Ø x 5/8" BOLT w/NUT AND WASHER
an 5/16"0 x 2" DOWEL
ai 1/4"Ø x 2 7/8" DOWEL
af 1/4"Ø x 7 1/4" THRD. ROD w/2 NUTS AND WASHERS
1"
5/16"
1/2"
1/2"
2 1/2"
1 1/2"
1/2"
DRILL 7/16"Ø HOLES 1/4" DEEP
ak 1/4"Ø WASH. 8 pcs.
ao 7/16"Ø x 1" DOWEL 2 pcs.
1/2"
1/4"
ap 5/16"Ø x 2" DOWEL
al 1 1/2"Ø x 7/16" DRILL 3/16"Ø AND 1/4"Ø HOLES THRU
aq 1"Ø FURNITURE PLUG
am 1/8"Ø x 7/8" BOLT w/NUT AND WASHER
ar 1"Ø x 3/8" DOWEL
bf 3/16"Ø SCREW EYE. 2 pcs.
be 3/16"Ø SCREW HOOK 2 pcs.
as 3/8"Ø CLASP HOOK
at 1/2"Ø x 4 1/2" DOWEL
au 2"Ø x 5" DOWEL DRILL 1"Ø AND 7/16"Ø HOLES 1/4" DEEP
2 1/2"
bg 18" BRASS JEWELER CHAIN 6 LINKS PER INCH
av 5/16" x 2 5/8" SQ. DRILL 2"Ø HOLE THRU 2 pcs.
aw 3/4" x 2 5/8" x 4 1/4" DRILL 1/2"Ø HOLE 3/8" DEEP
3/8"
1/2"
1/2"
bh 1/16"Ø BOLT w/nut
ax 2 1/4"Ø x 7/8" DRILL 7/16"Ø HOLE THRU 2 pcs.
bb 7/16"Ø x 1 1/2" DOWEL. MITER @ 25°
2 1/8"
STEERING DETAIL (BOTTOM)
ba 3/4" x 1" x 2 5/8" DRILL 1/2"Ø HOLE THRU
bc 3/16"Ø x 1/2" DOWEL
av 7/16"Ø FURNITURE PLUG - 2 pcs.
az 7/16"Ø x 3 3/4" DOWEL
bd 1/4"Ø x 1/2" DOWEL

BULLDOZER

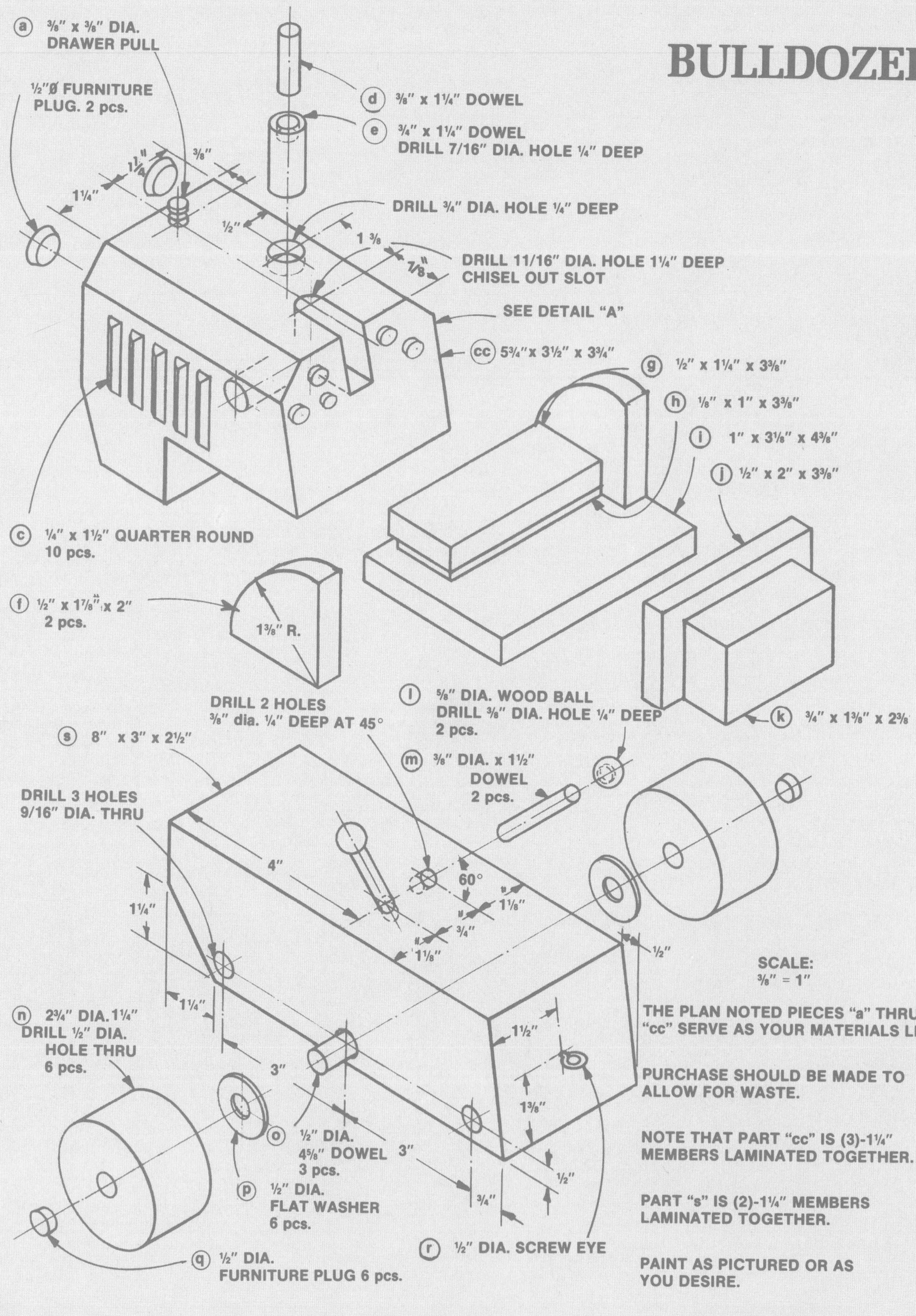

a 3/8" x 3/8" DIA. DRAWER PULL
1/2"Ø FURNITURE PLUG. 2 pcs.
1 1/4"
1 1/4"
3/8"
1/2"
d 3/8" x 1 1/4" DOWEL
e 3/4" x 1 1/4" DOWEL DRILL 7/16" DIA. HOLE 1/4" DEEP
DRILL 3/4" DIA. HOLE 1/4" DEEP
1 3/8
7/8"
DRILL 11/16" DIA. HOLE 1 1/4" DEEP CHISEL OUT SLOT
SEE DETAIL "A"
cc 5 3/4" x 3 1/2" x 3 3/4"
g 1/2" x 1 1/4" x 3 3/8"
h 1/8" x 1" x 3 3/8"
i 1" x 3 1/8" x 4 3/8"
j 1/2" x 2" x 3 3/8"
c 1/4" x 1 1/2" QUARTER ROUND 10 pcs.
f 1/2" x 1 7/8" x 2" 2 pcs.
1 3/8" R.
DRILL 2 HOLES 3/8" dia. 1/4" DEEP AT 45°
l 5/8" DIA. WOOD BALL DRILL 3/8" DIA. HOLE 1/4" DEEP 2 pcs.
k 3/4" x 1 3/8" x 2 3/8
s 8" x 3" x 2 1/2"
m 3/8" DIA. x 1 1/2" DOWEL 2 pcs.
DRILL 3 HOLES 9/16" DIA. THRU
4"
60°
1 1/8"
3/4"
1 1/8"
1 1/4"
1/2"
1 1/4"
n 2 3/4" DIA. 1 1/4" DRILL 1/2" DIA. HOLE THRU 6 pcs.
3"
1 1/2"
1 3/8"
o 1/2" DIA. 4 5/8" DOWEL 3 pcs.
3"
1/2"
3/4"
p 1/2" DIA. FLAT WASHER 6 pcs.
r 1/2" DIA. SCREW EYE
q 1/2" DIA. FURNITURE PLUG 6 pcs.

SCALE:
3/8" = 1"

THE PLAN NOTED PIECES "a" THRU "cc" SERVE AS YOUR MATERIALS LIST

PURCHASE SHOULD BE MADE TO ALLOW FOR WASTE.

NOTE THAT PART "cc" IS (3)-1 1/4" MEMBERS LAMINATED TOGETHER.

PART "s" IS (2)-1 1/4" MEMBERS LAMINATED TOGETHER.

PAINT AS PICTURED OR AS YOU DESIRE.

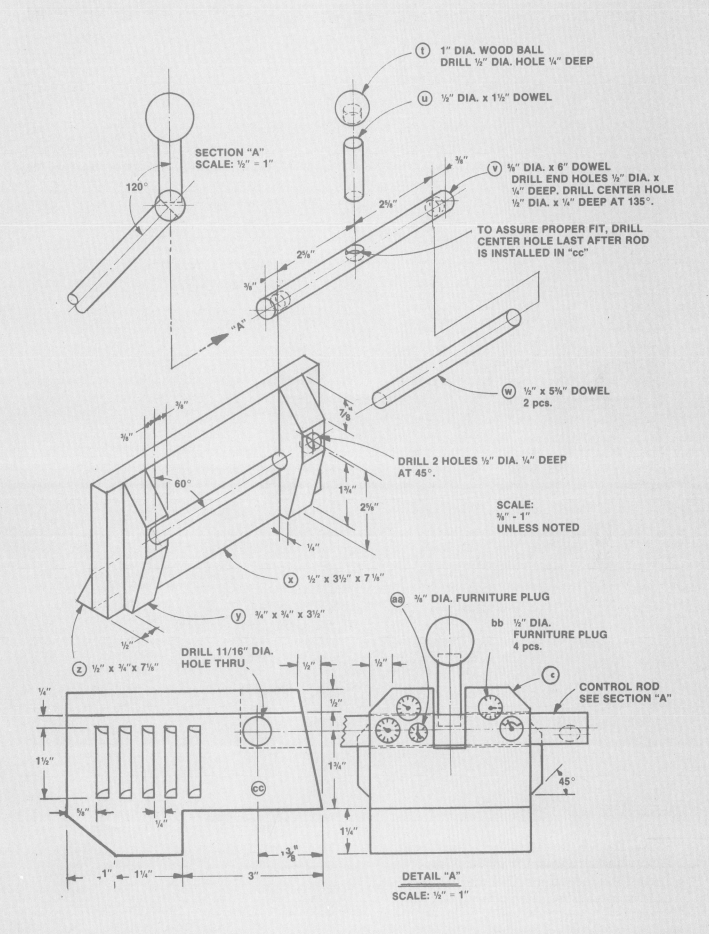

SECTION "A"
SCALE: ½" = 1"

120°

120°

t 1" DIA. WOOD BALL
   DRILL ½" DIA. HOLE ¼" DEEP

u ½" DIA. x 1½" DOWEL

v ⅝" DIA. x 6" DOWEL
   DRILL END HOLES ½" DIA. x
   ¼" DEEP. DRILL CENTER HOLE
   ½" DIA. x ¼" DEEP AT 135°.

TO ASSURE PROPER FIT, DRILL
CENTER HOLE LAST AFTER ROD
IS INSTALLED IN "cc"

⅜"

2⅝"

2⅝"

⅜"

"A"

w ½" x 5⅝" DOWEL
   2 pcs.

⅜"

⅜"

7/8

60°

DRILL 2 HOLES ½" DIA. ¼" DEEP
AT 45°.

1¾"

2⅝"

¼"

SCALE:
⅜" - 1"
UNLESS NOTED

x ½" x 3½" x 7⅛"

y ¾" x ¾" x 3½"

½"

z ½" x ¾" x 7⅛"

DRILL 11/16" DIA.
HOLE THRU

¼"

1½"

⅝"

¼"

1"   1¼"

3"

3/8"

½"   ½"

½"

1¾"

1¼"

cc

aa ⅜" DIA. FURNITURE PLUG

bb ½" DIA.
    FURNITURE PLUG
    4 pcs.

c

CONTROL ROD
SEE SECTION "A"

45°

DETAIL "A"

SCALE: ½" = 1"

TOW TRUCK
Heavy duty twin-stack truck with a
spring-loaded winch lock that will
hold a towed vehicle in any position.
Size: 17″ long, 7″ wide.

TOW TRUCK

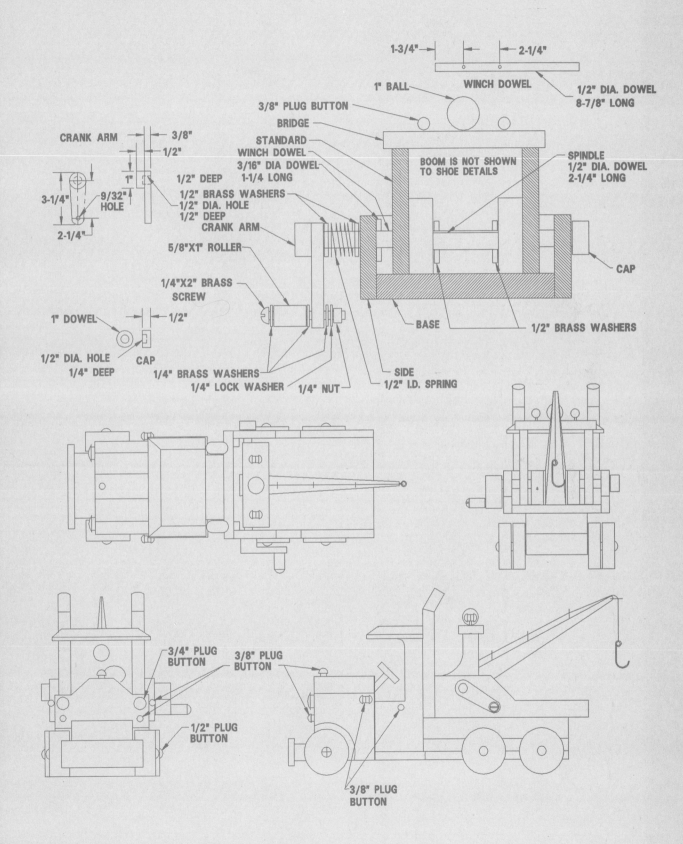

1-3/4"   2-1/4"

WINCH DOWEL

1" BALL

1/2" DIA. DOWEL
8-7/8" LONG

3/8" PLUG BUTTON

BRIDGE

CRANK ARM   3/8"

STANDARD
WINCH DOWEL

1/2"

3/16" DIA DOWEL
1-1/4 LONG

1"

1/2" DEEP

SPINDLE
1/2" DIA. DOWEL
2-1/4" LONG

BOOM IS NOT SHOWN
TO SHOE DETAILS

3-1/4"

9/32"
HOLE

1/2" BRASS WASHERS
1/2" DIA. HOLE
1/2" DEEP

CRANK ARM

2-1/4"

5/8"X1" ROLLER

CAP

1/4"X2" BRASS
SCREW

1" DOWEL

1/2"

1/2" DIA. HOLE
1/4" DEEP

CAP

BASE

1/2" BRASS WASHERS

1/4" BRASS WASHERS

1/4" LOCK WASHER   1/4" NUT

SIDE
1/2" I.D. SPRING

3/4" PLUG
BUTTON

3/8" PLUG
BUTTON

1/2" PLUG
BUTTON

3/8" PLUG
BUTTON

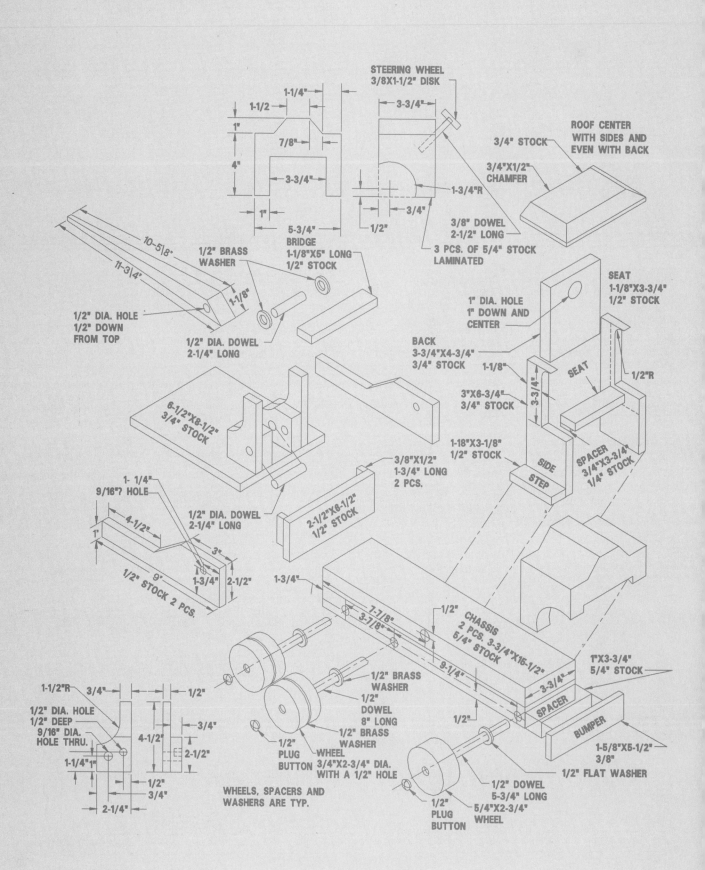

STEERING WHEEL
3/8X1-1/2" DISK

1-1/4"

1-1/2

1"

7/8"

4"

3-3/4"

1"

5-3/4"
BRIDGE
1-1/8"X5" LONG
1/2" STOCK

3-3/4"

1-3/4"R

3/4"

1/2"

ROOF CENTER
WITH SIDES AND
EVEN WITH BACK

3/4" STOCK

3/4"X1/2"
CHAMFER

3/8" DOWEL
2-1/2" LONG

3 PCS. OF 5/4" STOCK
LAMINATED

10-5|8"

11-3|4"

1-1/8"

1/2" BRASS
WASHER

1/2" DIA. HOLE
1/2" DOWN
FROM TOP

1/2" DIA. DOWEL
2-1/4" LONG

SEAT
1-1/8"X3-3/4"
1/2" STOCK

1" DIA. HOLE
1" DOWN AND
CENTER

BACK
3-3/4"X4-3/4"
3/4" STOCK

1-1/8"

SEAT

1/2"R

3"X6-3/4"
3/4" STOCK

3-3/4"

6-1/2"X8-1/2"
3/4" STOCK

1-18"X3-1/8"
1/2" STOCK

SPACER
3/4"X3-3/4"
1/4" STOCK

SIDE

STEP

1- 1/4"

9/16"7 HOLE

4-1/2"

1"

3"

9"

1-3/4"

2-1/2"

1/2" STOCK 2 PCS.

1/2" DIA. DOWEL
2-1/4" LONG

3/8"X1/2"
1-3/4" LONG
2 PCS.

2-1/2"X6-1/2"
1/2" STOCK

1-3/4"

1/2" CHASSIS
2 PCS, 3-3/4"X16-1/2"
5/4" STOCK

7-7/8"

3-7/8"

9-1/4"

3-3/4"

1"X3-3/4"
5/4" STOCK

SPACER

1-1/2"R

3/4"

1/2"

1/2" DIA. HOLE
1/2" DEEP
9/16" DIA.
HOLE THRU.

4-1/2"

3/4"

2-1/2"

1-1/4"

1"

1/2"

3/4"

2-1/4"

1/2" BRASS
WASHER

1/2"
DOWEL
8" LONG

1/2" BRASS
WASHER

1/2"
PLUG
BUTTON

WHEEL
3/4"X2-3/4" DIA.
WITH A 1/2" HOLE

WHEELS, SPACERS AND
WASHERS ARE TYP.

1/2"

1/2"
PLUG
BUTTON

1/2" DOWEL
5-3/4" LONG

5/4"X2-3/4"
WHEEL

BUMPER

1-5/8"X5-1/2"
3/8"

1/2" FLAT WASHER

62

RYAN'S RANCH

Ryan's animals always gather at the barn at feeding time. Each one has a home in the barn, and they enter through the sliding doors. The main floor has horse stalls and pens. The second floor loft has doors on each end that fold down, and is also accessible by lifting the top hinged roof panel. Size: 18" long, 13" wide, 14" high.

RYAN'S RANCH

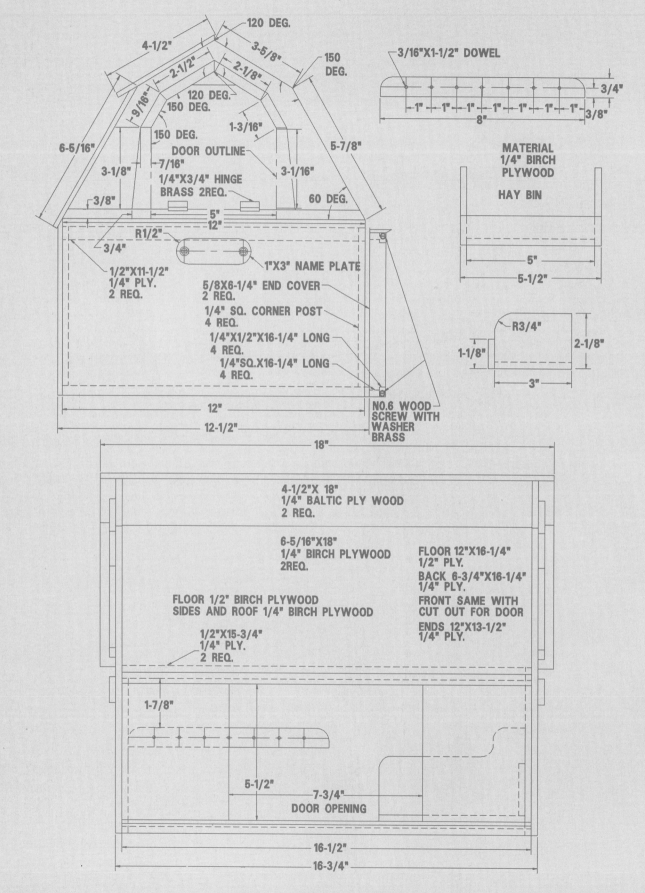

120 DEG.

4-1/2"   3-5/8"

150 DEG.

3/16"X1-1/2" DOWEL

3/4"

2-1/2"   2-1/8"

120 DEG.

150 DEG.

9/16"

1-3/16"

1"—1"—1"—1"—1"—1"—1"
8"
3/8"

150 DEG.

6-5/16"

150 DEG.

5-7/8"

MATERIAL
1/4" BIRCH
PLYWOOD

HAY BIN

DOOR OUTLINE

3-1/8"

7/16"

3-1/16"

1/4"X3/4" HINGE
BRASS 2REQ.

3/8"

60 DEG.

5"   12"

5"

R1/2"

5-1/2"

3/4"

1"X3" NAME PLATE

1/2"X11-1/2"
1/4" PLY.
2 REQ.

5/8X6-1/4" END COVER
2 REQ.

R3/4"

2-1/8"

1/4" SQ. CORNER POST
4 REQ.

1-1/8"

1/4"X1/2"X16-1/4" LONG
4 REQ.

3"

1/4"SQ.X16-1/4" LONG
4 REQ.

NO.6 WOOD
SCREW WITH
WASHER
BRASS

12"

12-1/2"

18"

4-1/2"X 18"
1/4" BALTIC PLY WOOD
2 REQ.

6-5/16"X18"
1/4" BIRCH PLYWOOD
2REQ.

FLOOR 12"X16-1/4"
1/2" PLY.

BACK 6-3/4"X16-1/4"
1/4" PLY.

FLOOR 1/2" BIRCH PLYWOOD
SIDES AND ROOF 1/4" BIRCH PLYWOOD

FRONT SAME WITH
CUT OUT FOR DOOR

ENDS 12"X13-1/2"
1/4" PLY.

1/2"X15-3/4"
1/4" PLY.
2 REQ.

1-7/8"

5-1/2"

7-3/4"

DOOR OPENING

16-1/2"

16-3/4"

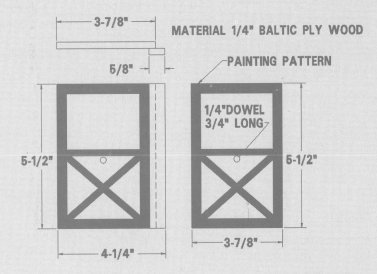

MATERIAL 1/4" BALTIC PLY WOOD

3-7/8"

5/8"

PAINTING PATTERN

1/4"DOWEL 3/4" LONG

5-1/2"

5-1/2"

4-1/4"

3-7/8"

MATERIAL 1/4" BALTIC PLY WOOD

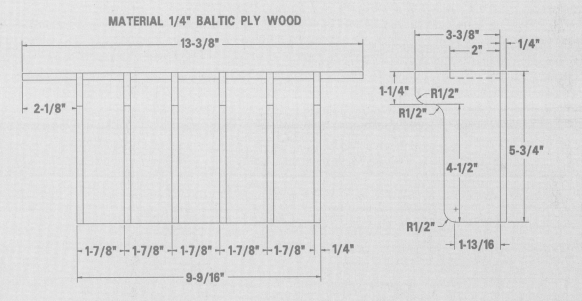

13-3/8"

2-1/8"

1-7/8" 1-7/8" 1-7/8" 1-7/8" 1-7/8" 1/4"

9-9/16"

3-3/8"

2"

1/4"

1-1/4" R1/2"

R1/2"

5-3/4"

4-1/2"

R1/2"

1-13/16

MATERIAL 1/4" BALTIC PLY WOOD

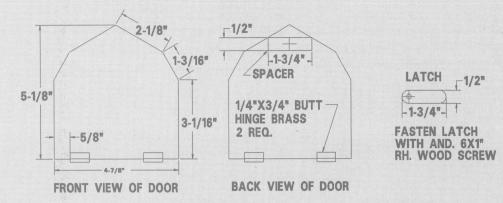

2-1/8"

1-3/16"

5-1/8"

5/8"

3-1/16"

4-7/8"

FRONT VIEW OF DOOR

1/2"

1-3/4"

SPACER

1/4"X3/4" BUTT
HINGE BRASS
2 REQ.

BACK VIEW OF DOOR

LATCH

1/2"

1-3/4"

FASTEN LATCH
WITH AND. 6X1"
RH. WOOD SCREW

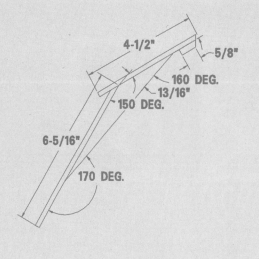

4-1/2"
5/8"
160 DEG.
13/16"
150 DEG.
6-5/16"
170 DEG.

5/8X11-7/8"
1/4" BALTIC PLY

135 DEG.

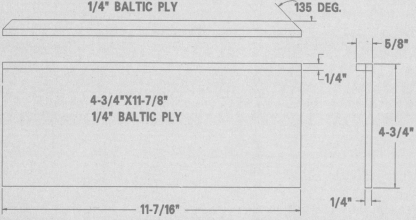

4-3/4"X11-7/8"
1/4" BALTIC PLY

5/8"
1/4"
4-3/4"
11-7/16"
1/4"

ROOF ASSY.

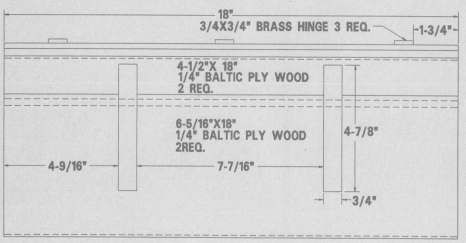

18"
3/4X3/4" BRASS HINGE 3 REQ.
1-3/4"

4-1/2"X 18"
1/4" BALTIC PLY WOOD
2 REQ.

6-5/16"X18"
1/4" BALTIC PLY WOOD
2REQ.

4-7/8"

4-9/16"
7-7/16"
3/4"

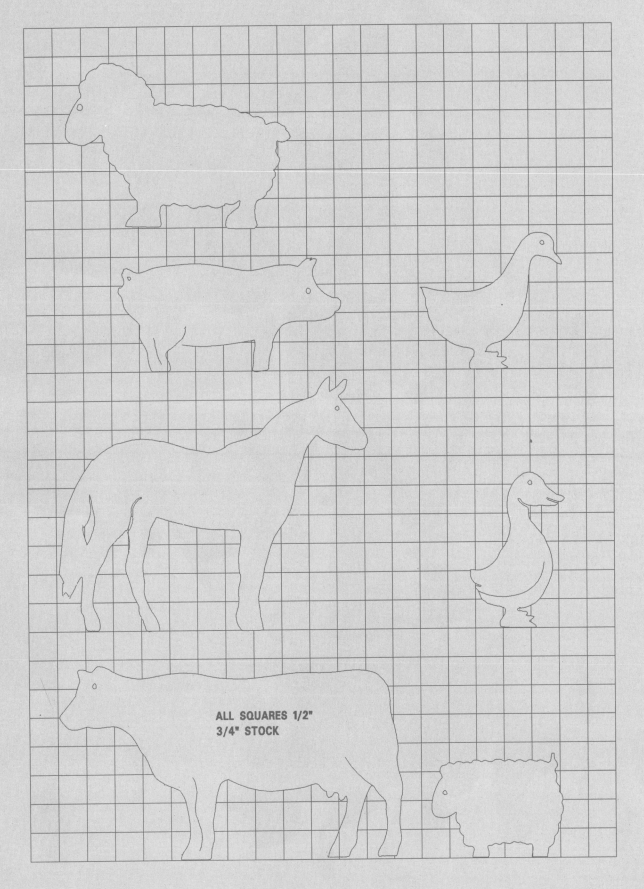

ALL SQUARES 1/2"
3/4" STOCK

FERRIS WHEEL
We don't think you'll find a toy like this anywhere else! Children head for this toy straight away. They enjoy giving all little people rides with a working hand crank. Plan includes patterns for people which are turned on a wood lathe. Size: 12″ x 14″, by 22″ high.

FERRIS WHEEL

PARTS OF ROOF AND SWINGS LEFT OFF TO SHOW DETAIL

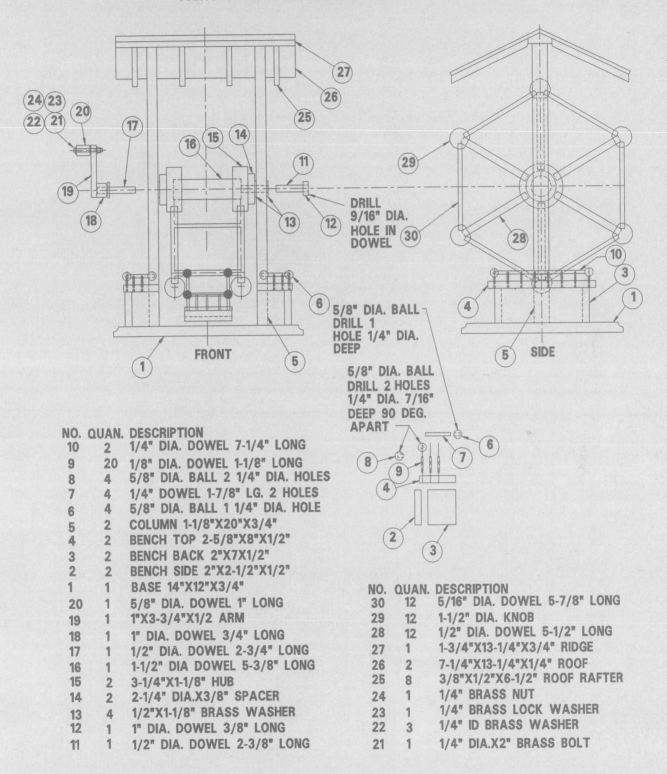

FRONT

SIDE

DRILL 9/16" DIA. HOLE IN DOWEL

5/8" DIA. BALL DRILL 1 HOLE 1/4" DIA. DEEP

5/8" DIA. BALL DRILL 2 HOLES 1/4" DIA. 7/16" DEEP 90 DEG. APART

NO.	QUAN.	DESCRIPTION
10	2	1/4" DIA. DOWEL 7-1/4" LONG
9	20	1/8" DIA. DOWEL 1-1/8" LONG
8	4	5/8" DIA. BALL 2 1/4" DIA. HOLES
7	4	1/4" DOWEL 1-7/8" LG. 2 HOLES
6	4	5/8" DIA. BALL 1 1/4" DIA. HOLE
5	2	COLUMN 1-1/8"X20"X3/4"
4	2	BENCH TOP 2-5/8"X8"X1/2"
3	2	BENCH BACK 2"X7X1/2"
2	2	BENCH SIDE 2"X2-1/2"X1/2"
1	1	BASE 14"X12"X3/4"
20	1	5/8" DIA. DOWEL 1" LONG
19	1	1"X3-3/4"X1/2 ARM
18	1	1" DIA. DOWEL 3/4" LONG
17	1	1/2" DIA. DOWEL 2-3/4" LONG
16	1	1-1/2" DIA DOWEL 5-3/8" LONG
15	2	3-1/4"X1-1/8" HUB
14	2	2-1/4" DIA.X3/8" SPACER
13	4	1/2"X1-1/8" BRASS WASHER
12	1	1" DIA. DOWEL 3/8" LONG
11	1	1/2" DIA. DOWEL 2-3/8" LONG

NO.	QUAN.	DESCRIPTION
30	12	5/16" DIA. DOWEL 5-7/8" LONG
29	12	1-1/2" DIA. KNOB
28	12	1/2" DIA. DOWEL 5-1/2" LONG
27	1	1-3/4"X13-1/4"X3/4" RIDGE
26	2	7-1/4"X13-1/4"X1/4" ROOF
25	8	3/8"X1/2"X6-1/2" ROOF RAFTER
24	1	1/4" BRASS NUT
23	1	1/4" BRASS LOCK WASHER
22	3	1/4" ID BRASS WASHER
21	1	1/4" DIA.X2" BRASS BOLT

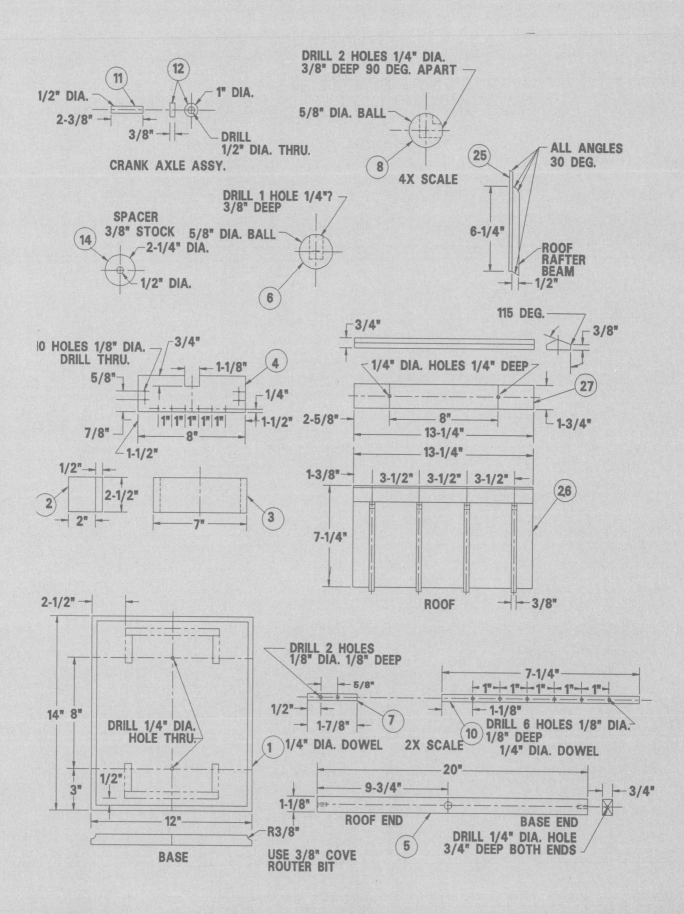

CRANK AXLE ASSY.

1/2" DIA.
2-3/8"
3/8"
1" DIA.
DRILL 1/2" DIA. THRU.
11
12

DRILL 2 HOLES 1/4" DIA. 3/8" DEEP 90 DEG. APART
5/8" DIA. BALL
4X SCALE
8

25
ALL ANGLES 30 DEG.
6-1/4"
ROOF RAFTER BEAM
1/2"

SPACER
3/8" STOCK
2-1/4" DIA.
1/2" DIA.
14

DRILL 1 HOLE 1/4"?
3/8" DEEP
5/8" DIA. BALL
6

10 HOLES 1/8" DIA. DRILL THRU.
3/4"
5/8"
1-1/8"
1/4"
1" 1" 1" 1" 1"
1-1/2"
8"
7/8"
1-1/2"
4

3/4"
1/4" DIA. HOLES 1/4" DEEP
8"
13-1/4"
2-5/8"
115 DEG.
3/8"
1-3/4"
27

13-1/4"
1-3/8"
3-1/2" 3-1/2" 3-1/2"
7-1/4"
3/8"
26
ROOF

1/2"
2"
2-1/2"
2

7"
3

2-1/2"
14" 8"
DRILL 1/4" DIA. HOLE THRU.
1/2"
3"
12"
R3/8"
BASE
USE 3/8" COVE ROUTER BIT
1

DRILL 2 HOLES 1/8" DIA. 1/8" DEEP
5/8"
1/2"
1-7/8"
1/4" DIA. DOWEL
7
2X SCALE

7-1/4"
1" 1" 1" 1" 1"
1-1/8"
DRILL 6 HOLES 1/8" DIA. 1/8" DEEP
1/4" DIA. DOWEL
10

20"
9-3/4"
3/4"
1-1/8"
ROOF END
BASE END
DRILL 1/4" DIA. HOLE 3/4" DEEP BOTH ENDS
5

70

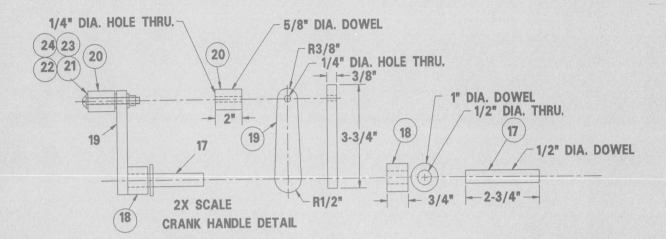

1/4" DIA. HOLE THRU.

⑳ ⑳ ⑳ ⑳

5/8" DIA. DOWEL

⑳

R3/8"

1/4" DIA. HOLE THRU.

3/8"

1" DIA. DOWEL

1/2" DIA. THRU.

⑱ ⑰

1/2" DIA. DOWEL

19

17

2"

19

3-3/4"

R1/2"

3/4"

2-3/4"

18

2X SCALE
CRANK HANDLE DETAIL

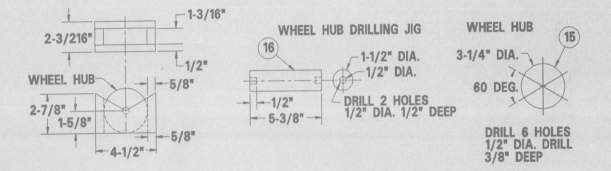

1-3/16"

2-3/216"

1/2"

WHEEL HUB

5/8"

2-7/8"

1-5/8"

5/8"

4-1/2"

WHEEL HUB DRILLING JIG

⑯

1-1/2" DIA.

1/2" DIA.

1/2"

5-3/8"

DRILL 2 HOLES
1/2" DIA. 1/2" DEEP

WHEEL HUB

⑮

3-1/4" DIA.

60 DEG.

DRILL 6 HOLES
1/2" DIA. DRILL
3/8" DEEP

BE CAREFULL TO DRILL HOLE THRU FERRIS WHEEL HUBS AND AXLE AS
STRAIGHT AS POSSIBLE IN ORDER TO KEEP THE WHEEL LEVEL AND ALLOW IT
TO ROTATE PROPERLY.

MAKING THE WHEEL HUB DRILLING JIG

USING FULL SIZE FRONT VIEW OF JIG, TRACE ANGLE OF CUTS ONTO WOOD
PIECES. AFTER COMPLETING CUTS ALIGN THE FOUR PIECES AS SHOWN.
NOTE: CHECK THE FIT OF THE WHEEL HUB IN THE JIG BEFORE GLUING AND
NAILING THE JIG TOGETHER. THE WHEEL HUB SHOULD TURN FREELY BUT
WITHOUT ANY WOBBLE.

USING THE WHEEL HUB DRILLING JIG.

FIRST DRAW WITH PENCIL THREE DIAGONALS 60 DEG. APART ACROSS
WHEEL HUB AS SHOWN.

INSERT THE WHEEL HUB IN THE JIG AS SHOWN. MATCH A DIAGONAL LINE
ALONG THE TOP EDGE OF THE JIG LEAVING ONE DIAGONAL IN A VERTICAL
POSITION. DRILL A 1/2" DIA. HOLE 3/8" DEEP FOR WHEEL SPOKE,
ROTATE THE WHEEL HUB TO MATCH UP THE NEXT DIAGONAL AND REPEAT
DRILLING (ALL HOLES ARE 60 DEG. APART) DRILL 6 HOLES.
AFTER YOU HAVE FINISHED DRILLING THE HUB FOR WHEEL SPOKES, DRILL A
1/2" HOLE INTO THE HUB CENTER FOR THE CRANK AXLE AND A 1-1/2" DIA.
HOLE 1/2" DEEP TO ACCOMMODATE THE END OF THE WHEEL AXLE.

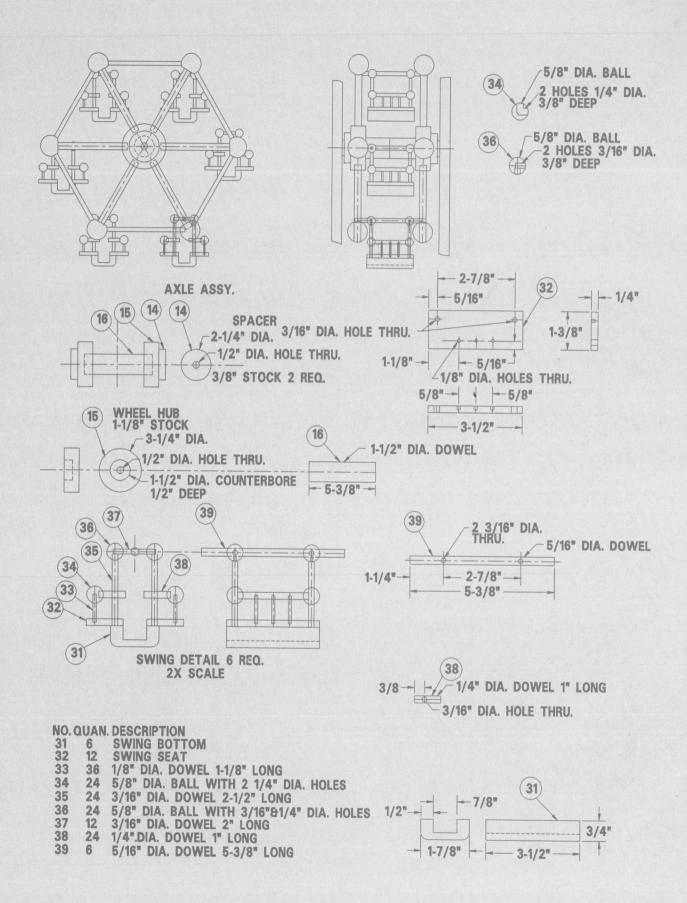

AXLE ASSY.

(16) (15) (14) (14)

SPACER
2-1/4" DIA. 3/16" DIA. HOLE THRU.
1/2" DIA. HOLE THRU.
3/8" STOCK 2 REQ.

(34) 5/8" DIA. BALL
2 HOLES 1/4" DIA.
3/8" DEEP

(36) 5/8" DIA. BALL
2 HOLES 3/16" DIA.
3/8" DEEP

2-7/8"
5/16"
(32)
1/4"
1-3/8"
1-1/8"
5/16"
1/8" DIA. HOLES THRU.
5/8"   5/8"
3-1/2"

(15) **WHEEL HUB**
1-1/8" STOCK
3-1/4" DIA.
1/2" DIA. HOLE THRU.
1-1/2" DIA. COUNTERBORE
1/2" DEEP

(16) 1-1/2" DIA. DOWEL
5-3/8"

(36) (37) (39)
(35)
(34)
(33)
(32)
(31)

SWING DETAIL 6 REQ.
2X SCALE

(39) 2 3/16" DIA. THRU.
5/16" DIA. DOWEL
1-1/4"
2-7/8"
5-3/8"

(38)
3/8   1/4" DIA. DOWEL 1" LONG
3/16" DIA. HOLE THRU.

NO.	QUAN.	DESCRIPTION
31	6	SWING BOTTOM
32	12	SWING SEAT
33	36	1/8" DIA. DOWEL 1-1/8" LONG
34	24	5/8" DIA. BALL WITH 2 1/4" DIA. HOLES
35	24	3/16" DIA. DOWEL 2-1/2" LONG
36	24	5/8" DIA. BALL WITH 3/16"&1/4" DIA. HOLES
37	12	3/16" DIA. DOWEL 2" LONG
38	24	1/4".DIA. DOWEL 1" LONG
39	6	5/16" DIA. DOWEL 5-3/8" LONG

(31)
1/2"   7/8"
3/4"
1-7/8"   3-1/2"

NOTES:

THE FERRIS WHEEL PROJECT CONSISTS OF MAIN SUB-ASSEMBLIES:
BENCHES (2), SWINGS (6), FERRIS WHEEL, AND ROOF. CONSTRUCTION
OF THE THESE ASSEMBLIES CAN BE IN ANY ORDER. HOWEVER, IT IS
SUGGESTED THAT YOU PREPARE THE PLATFORM PIECE AND DRILLING
JIGS FIRST.
STUDY THE PLANS CAREFULLY BEFORE YOU BEGIN.
TEST ALL MOVABLE PARTS FOR FREEDOM OF FIT . ASSEMBLE ONLY
WHEN PARTS FIT WITHOUT BINDING.
SAND SURFACES AS NEEDED. ANY PLACE WHERE FINISHING NAILS
WERE NEEDED, THE NAILS SHOULD BE SET. PUTTY NAIL HOLES WHEN
FINISHING.
TO FINISH USE 2 COATS OF SANDING SEALER 1 COAT OF POLY-
URETHANE GLOSS VARNISH. SANDING BEFORE AND BETWEEN COATS.
PAINT THE WOODEN BALLS VARIOUS COLORS OF YOUR CHOICE.

1-1/2" DIA. THRU

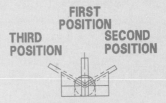

FIRST
POSITION
THIRD   SECOND
POSITION   POSITION

KNOB DRILLING JIG
FRONT VIEW

METHOD OF DRILLING WOODEN BALLS

NOTE: THAT ALL THE WOODEN BALLS ON THE
SWING AND HALF ON BENCH FORM AN ELBOW
JOINT, MAKING THE HOLES DRILLED AT 90 DEG.
ANGLES TO EACH OTHER. SECURE BALL BETWEEN
THE JAWS OF A VISE. DRILL THE REQUIRED SIZE
HOLE THEN INSERT DOWEL. USING THE DOWEL
AS A MARKER. REPOSITION THE BALL SO THE
DOWEL IS PARALLEL TO THE TOP EDGE OF THE
VISE JAWS. THEN DRILL NEXT HOLE THE
REQUIRED SIZE.
NOTE NOT ALL DOWELS ARE THE SAME SIZE.
YOU MAY NEED TO CHANGE DRILL SIZE TO
MATCH DOWELS.
NOTE ONE OF THE HOLES MAY NOT BE DRILLED
THRU. CHECK THE DRAWINGS CAREFULLY.

MAKING THE KNOB DRILLING JIG

USING FRONT VIEW OF JIG DRAW ANGLE OF CUTS
ONTO WOOD PIECES. AFTER CUTTING, ALIGN THE
THREE PIECES AS SHOWN AND GLUE, THEN DRILL
A 1-1/2" DIA. HOLE THRU THE CENTER FROM THE
TOP USING A HOLE CUTTER.

USING THE KNOB DRILLING JIG

PLACE THE DRAWER KNOB IN THE JIG WITH FLAT
SURFACE UP. DRILL 1/2" DIA. HOLE 3/8" DEEP FOR
WHEEL SPOKES, INSERT SPOKE AND TURN KNOB
TO THE 2ND POSITION. DRILL 1/2" DIA. HOLE 3/16"
DEEP FOR THE WHEEL RIM TIE. TURN TO 3RD
POSITION AND REPEAT FOR SECOND WHEEL RIM
TIE. ALL HOLES ARE 60 DEG. APART.

MATERIALS:

AMOUNT		DESCRIPTION
5	LF	1/8" DIA. DOWEL, BIRCH, FOR SWING & BENCH SEAT RAILING
6	LF	3/16" DIA. DOWEL, BIRCH, FOR SWING SEAT RAILING
.5	LF	1/4" DIA. DOWEL FOR ROOF SUPPORT POST
12	LF	5/16" DIA. DOWEL FOR FERRIS WHEEL AND SWING & BENCH, SEAT RAILING
8	LF	1/2" DIA. DOWEL FOR FERRIS WHEEL & CRANK AXLES
3	LF	1-1/2" DIA. DOWEL FOR FERRIS WHEEL AXLE
12		1-1/2" DIA. DRAWER KNOB FOR FERRIS WHEEL
56		5/8" DIA. BALL FOR SWING & BENCH SEATS
		1/4" X 1-3/8" MULLION, PINE FOR SWING SEATS
6	LF	1/2" X 2-1/2" PINE FOR ROOF BEAMS, BENCH SEATS & CRANK HANDLE
4	LF	1 X 2" PINE FOR ROOF SUPPORT POST, BEAMS & SWING BOTTOMS
2.5	LF	1 X 8" PINE FOR PLATFORM
.5	LF	1 X 4" PINE FOR SPACERS
.5	LF	2 X 4" PINE FOR WHEEL HUBS
4		1/2" I.D. BRASS FLAT WASHERS FOR AXLE
3		1/4" I.D. BRASS FLAT WASHER FOR CRANK HANDLE
1		1/4" I.D. BRASS LOCK WASHER FOR CRANK HANDLE
1		1/4" I.D. BRASS HEX. NUT FOR CRANK HANDLE
1		1/4" DIA. ROUND HEAD BOLT 2" LONG FOR CRANK HANDLE

AS NEEDED #14 WIRE BRAD, BRASS. 3/4" LONG FOR BENCH SEATS & CRANK HANDLE.
GLUE, FINISHING NAILS, PAINT & VARNISH AS NEEDED
IT MAY BE NECESSARY TO OBTAIN ADDITIONAL AMOUNTS DUE TO CONSTRUCTION WASTE.

1. Marina
2. Town Buildings
3. Sailboats
4. Power Boats
5. Work Boats
6. Stern Wheeler
7. Side Wheeler
8. Car Ferry

MYSTIC SEAPORT

Here the owner is captain and harbormaster of all that moves. Makes shipping schedules. Sells tickets for river boat rides. Directs cargo. Loads and unloads barges. Boats can be duplicated to enlarge the fleet. This marina can grow and grow and grow and will provide years of continuous enjoyment.

CAR FERRY

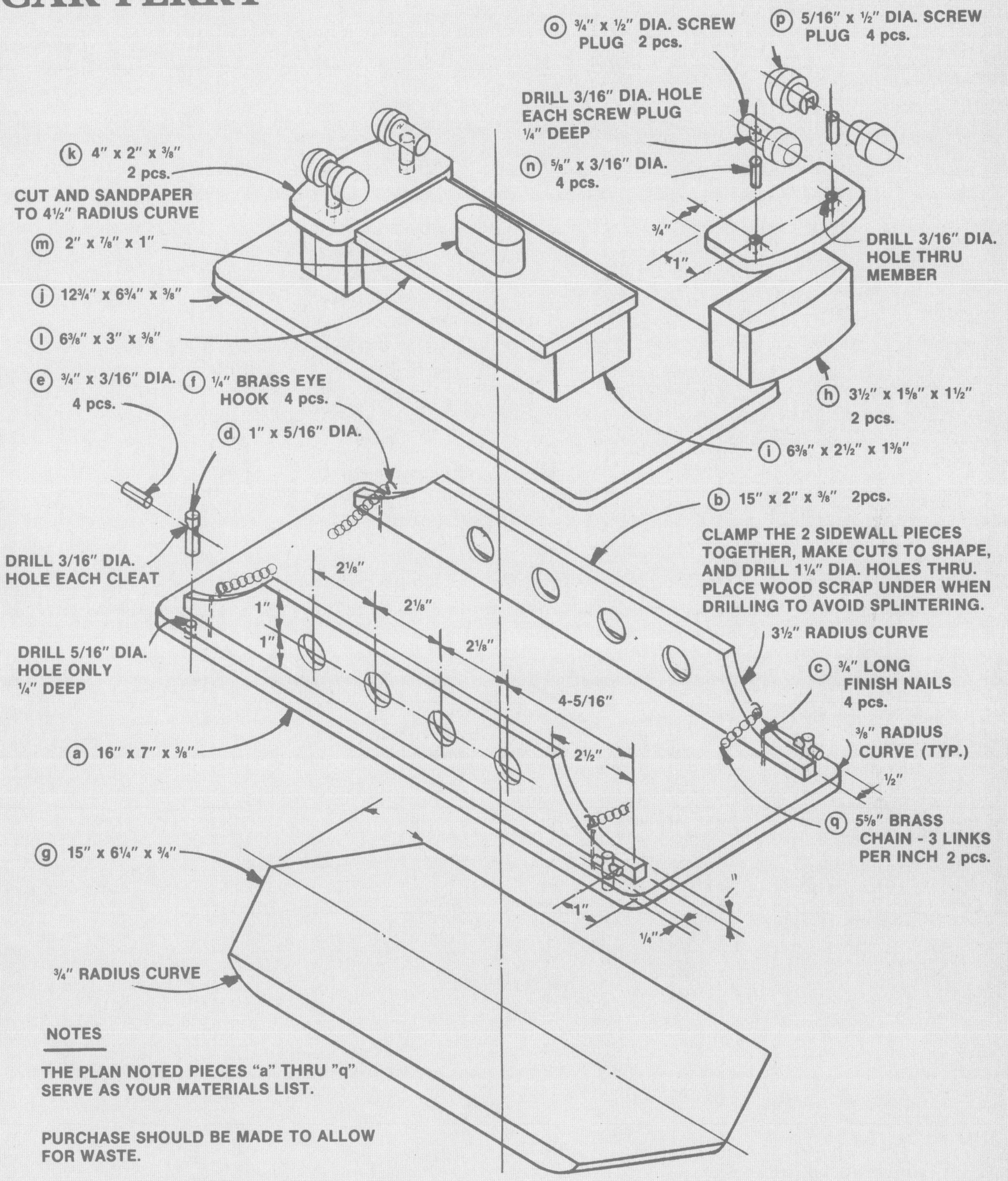

(o) ¾" x ½" DIA. SCREW PLUG 2 pcs.
(p) 5/16" x ½" DIA. SCREW PLUG 4 pcs.
DRILL 3/16" DIA. HOLE EACH SCREW PLUG ¼" DEEP
(k) 4" x 2" x ⅜" 2 pcs.
CUT AND SANDPAPER TO 4½" RADIUS CURVE
(n) ⅝" x 3/16" DIA. 4 pcs.
¾"
1"
(m) 2" x ⅞" x 1"
DRILL 3/16" DIA. HOLE THRU MEMBER
(j) 12¾" x 6¾" x ⅜"
(l) 6⅜" x 3" x ⅜"
(e) ¾" x 3/16" DIA. 4 pcs.
(f) ¼" BRASS EYE HOOK 4 pcs.
(h) 3½" x 1⅝" x 1½" 2 pcs.
(d) 1" x 5/16" DIA.
(i) 6⅜" x 2½" x 1⅜"
(b) 15" x 2" x ⅜" 2pcs.
CLAMP THE 2 SIDEWALL PIECES TOGETHER, MAKE CUTS TO SHAPE, AND DRILL 1¼" DIA. HOLES THRU. PLACE WOOD SCRAP UNDER WHEN DRILLING TO AVOID SPLINTERING.
DRILL 3/16" DIA. HOLE EACH CLEAT
2⅛"
2⅛"
1"
1"
2⅛"
3½" RADIUS CURVE
DRILL 5/16" DIA. HOLE ONLY ¼" DEEP
(c) ¾" LONG FINISH NAILS 4 pcs.
4-5/16"
⅜" RADIUS CURVE (TYP.)
(a) 16" x 7" x ⅜"
2½"
½"
(q) 5⅝" BRASS CHAIN - 3 LINKS PER INCH 2 pcs.
(g) 15" x 6¼" x ¾"
1"
¼"
¾" RADIUS CURVE

NOTES

THE PLAN NOTED PIECES "a" THRU "q" SERVE AS YOUR MATERIALS LIST.

PURCHASE SHOULD BE MADE TO ALLOW FOR WASTE.

ALL PARTS SUCH AS SCREW PLUGS FOR THE LIGHTS AND HORNS MAY BE PURCHASED AT ANY RETAIL HARDWARE STORE.

NOTE THAT PART "h" CONSISTS OF 1" and ⅝" THICK MEMBERS LAMINATED TOGETHER.
PART "i" CONSISTS OF TWO 1¼" THICK MEMBERS LAMINATED.

USE POLYURETHANE SEALER OVERALL.
PAINT AS PICTURED OR PER YOUR DESIRE.
USE TWO COATS SPAR WATERPROOF VARNISH (THIRD COAT TO BOAT BOTTOM).

SAILBOAT

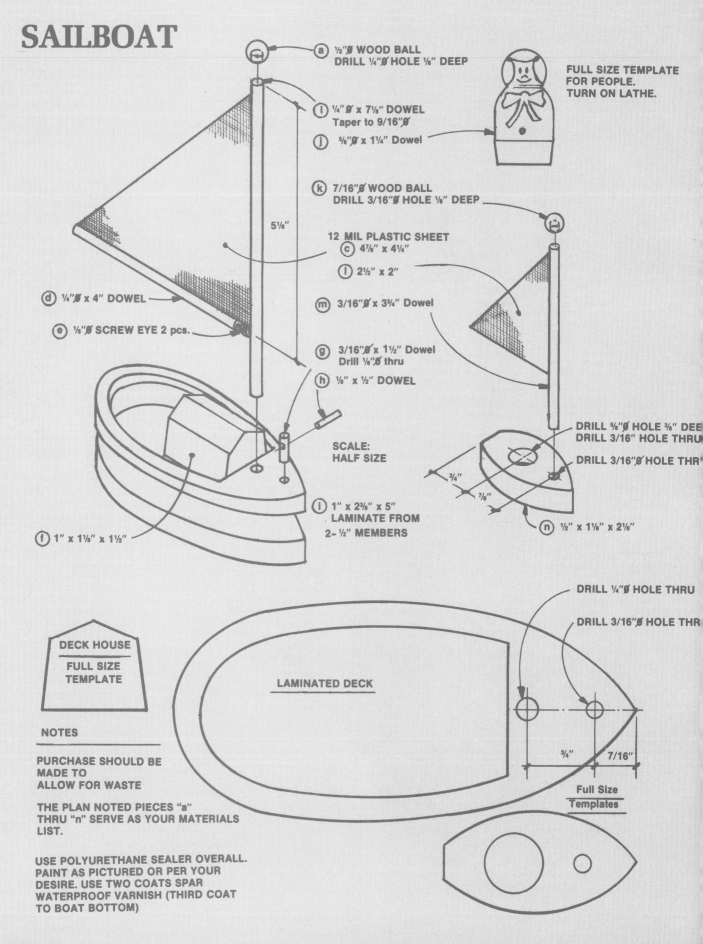

FULL SIZE TEMPLATE FOR PEOPLE. TURN ON LATHE.

(a) ½"∅ WOOD BALL
DRILL ¼"∅ HOLE ⅛" DEEP

(i) ¼"∅ x 7⅛" DOWEL
Taper to 9/16"∅

(j) ⅝"∅ x 1¼" Dowel

(k) 7/16"∅ WOOD BALL
DRILL 3/16"∅ HOLE ⅛" DEEP

12 MIL PLASTIC SHEET
(c) 4⅞" x 4¼"

(l) 2½" x 2"

(m) 3/16"∅ x 3¾" Dowel

5⅛"

(d) ¼"∅ x 4" DOWEL

(e) ⅛"∅ SCREW EYE 2 pcs.

(g) 3/16"∅ x 1½" Dowel
Drill ⅛"∅ thru

(h) ⅛" x ½" DOWEL

SCALE:
HALF SIZE

DRILL ⅝"∅ HOLE ¾" DEE
DRILL 3/16" HOLE THRU

DRILL 3/16"∅ HOLE THR

¾"

⅞"

(b) 1" x 2⅜" x 5"
LAMINATE FROM
2- ½" MEMBERS

(n) ½" x 1⅛" x 2⅛"

(f) 1" x 1⅛" x 1½"

DECK HOUSE

FULL SIZE TEMPLATE

DRILL ¼"∅ HOLE THRU

DRILL 3/16"∅ HOLE THR

LAMINATED DECK

¾"

7/16"

Full Size Templates

NOTES

PURCHASE SHOULD BE MADE TO ALLOW FOR WASTE

THE PLAN NOTED PIECES "a" THRU "n" SERVE AS YOUR MATERIALS LIST.

USE POLYURETHANE SEALER OVERALL. PAINT AS PICTURED OR PER YOUR DESIRE. USE TWO COATS SPAR WATERPROOF VARNISH (THIRD COAT TO BOAT BOTTOM)

MARINA HOME

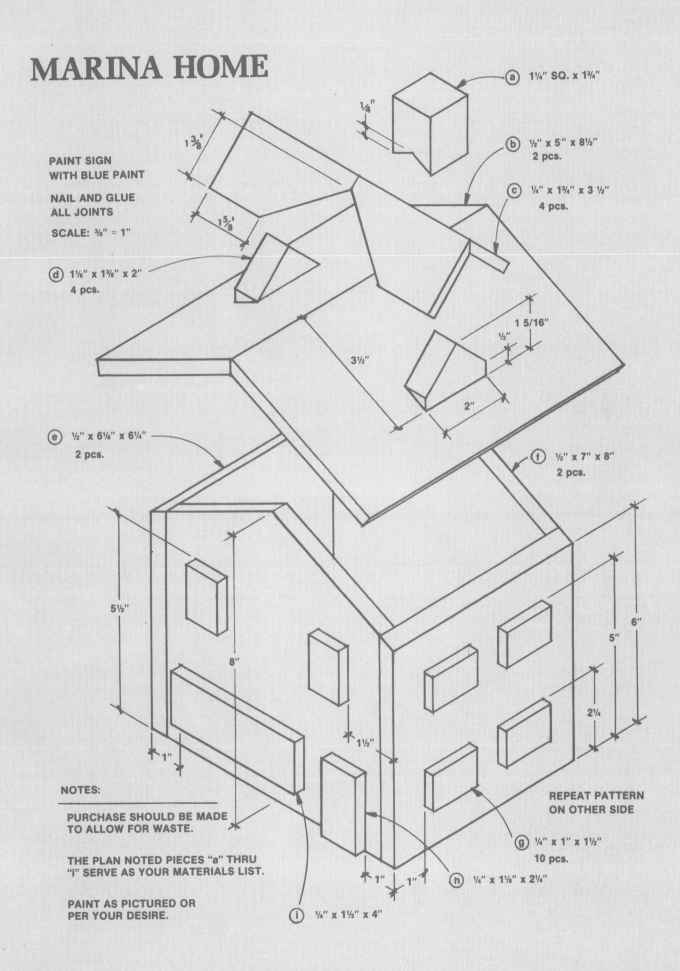

PAINT SIGN
WITH BLUE PAINT

NAIL AND GLUE
ALL JOINTS

SCALE: ⅜" = 1"

(a) 1¼" SQ. x 1¾"

1/4"

(b) ½" x 5" x 8½"
2 pcs.

(c) ¼" x 1¾" x 3 ½"
4 pcs.

(d) 1⅛" x 1⅜" x 2"
4 pcs.

1⅜"

1⅝"

1 5/16"

½"

3½"

2"

(e) ½" x 6⅛" x 6¼"
2 pcs.

(f) ½" x 7" x 8"
2 pcs.

5½"

8"

6"

5"

2¼"

1½"

1"

REPEAT PATTERN
ON OTHER SIDE

(g) ¼" x 1" x 1½"
10 pcs.

1"   1"

(h) ¼" x 1⅛" x 2¼"

NOTES:

PURCHASE SHOULD BE MADE
TO ALLOW FOR WASTE.

THE PLAN NOTED PIECES "a" THRU
"i" SERVE AS YOUR MATERIALS LIST.

PAINT AS PICTURED OR
PER YOUR DESIRE.

(i) ¼" x 1½" x 4"

79

BARGE

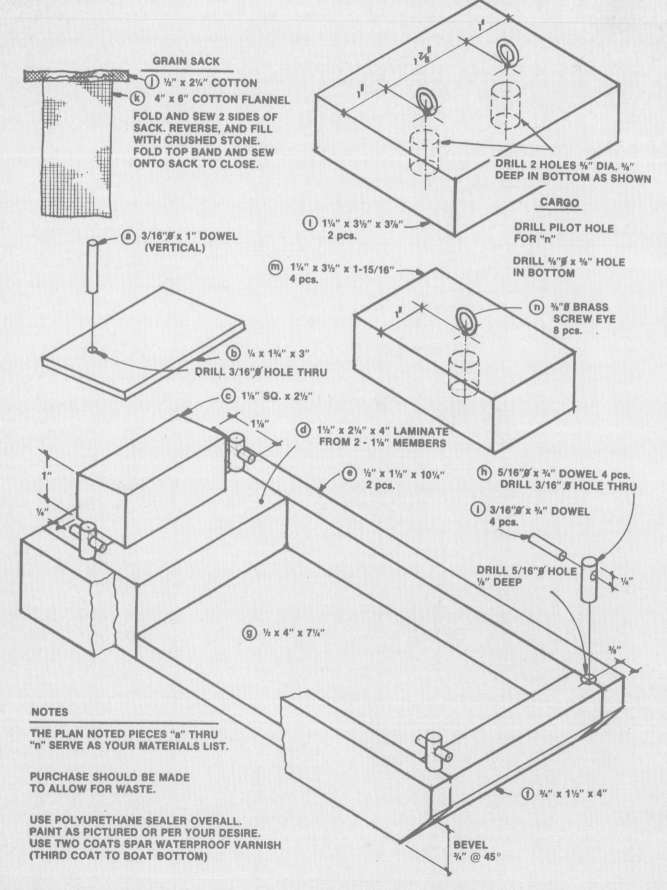

GRAIN SACK

ⓙ ½" x 2¼" COTTON
ⓚ 4" x 6" COTTON FLANNEL

FOLD AND SEW 2 SIDES OF
SACK. REVERSE, AND FILL
WITH CRUSHED STONE.
FOLD TOP BAND AND SEW
ONTO SACK TO CLOSE.

DRILL 2 HOLES ⅝" DIA. ⅝"
DEEP IN BOTTOM AS SHOWN

CARGO

DRILL PILOT HOLE
FOR "n"

DRILL ⅝"∅ x ⅝" HOLE
IN BOTTOM

ⓐ 3/16"∅ x 1" DOWEL
(VERTICAL)

ⓛ 1¼" x 3½" x 3⅞"
2 pcs.

ⓜ 1¼" x 3½" x 1-15/16"
4 pcs.

ⓝ ⅜"∅ BRASS
SCREW EYE
8 pcs.

ⓑ ¼ x 1¾" x 3"

DRILL 3/16"∅ HOLE THRU

ⓒ 1⅛" SQ. x 2½"

1⅛"

ⓓ 1½" x 2¼" x 4" LAMINATE
FROM 2 - 1⅛" MEMBERS

ⓔ ½" x 1½" x 10¼"
2 pcs.

ⓗ 5/16"∅ x ¾" DOWEL 4 pcs.
DRILL 3/16"∅ HOLE THRU

ⓘ 3/16"∅ x ¾" DOWEL
4 pcs.

1"

¼"

DRILL 5/16"∅ HOLE
⅛" DEEP

¼"

⅜"

ⓖ ½ x 4" x 7¼"

NOTES

THE PLAN NOTED PIECES "a" THRU
"n" SERVE AS YOUR MATERIALS LIST.

PURCHASE SHOULD BE MADE
TO ALLOW FOR WASTE.

USE POLYURETHANE SEALER OVERALL.
PAINT AS PICTURED OR PER YOUR DESIRE.
USE TWO COATS SPAR WATERPROOF VARNISH
(THIRD COAT TO BOAT BOTTOM)

ⓕ ¾" x 1½" x 4"

BEVEL
¾" @ 45°

MARINA DOCK

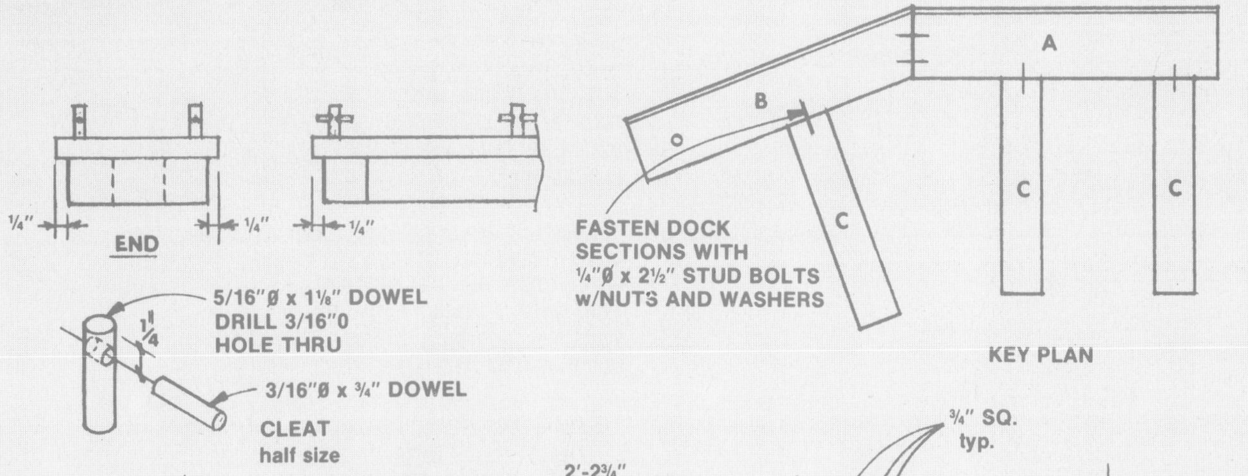

1/4"
1/4"
1/4"
1/4"
END
5/16"Ø x 1 1/8" DOWEL
DRILL 3/16"0
HOLE THRU
1/4
3/16"Ø x 3/4" DOWEL
CLEAT
half size
FASTEN DOCK
SECTIONS WITH
1/4"Ø x 2 1/2" STUD BOLTS
w/NUTS AND WASHERS
A
B
C
C
C
KEY PLAN

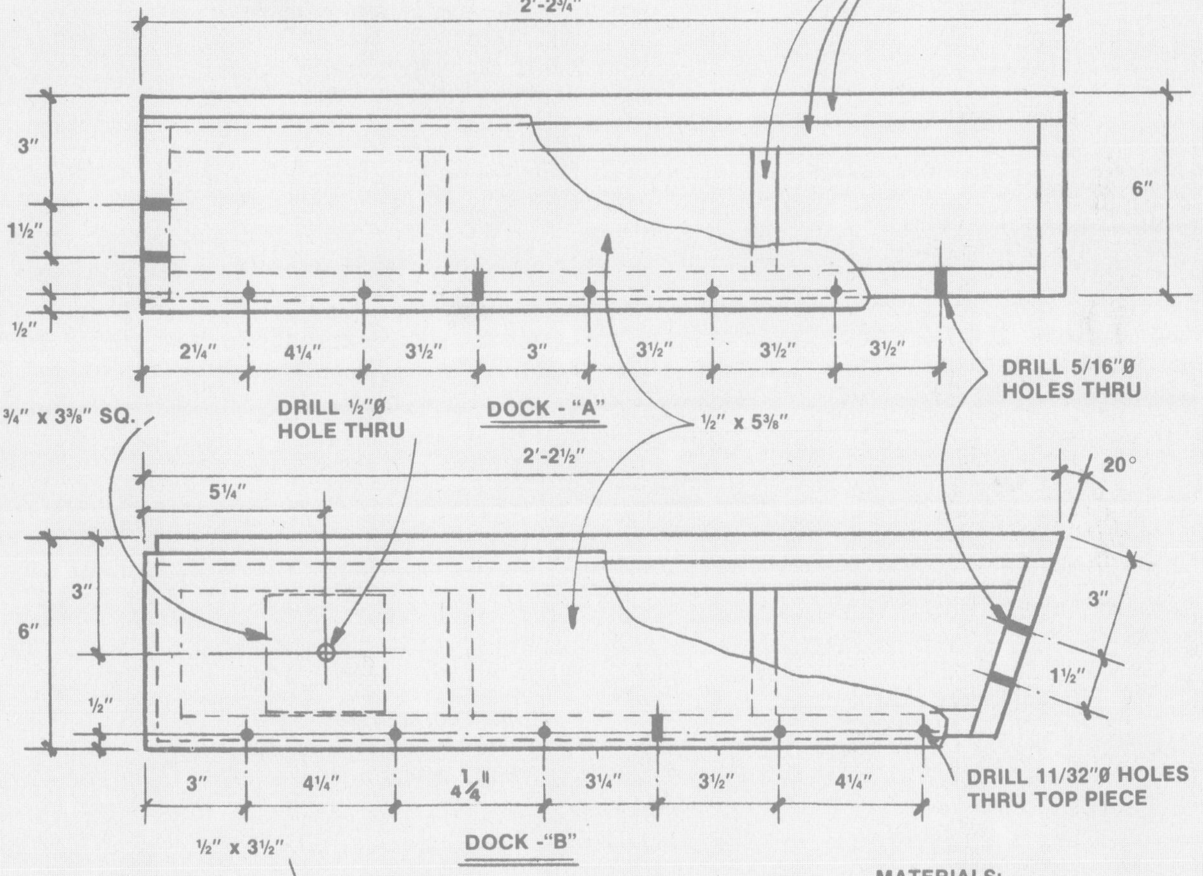

3/4" SQ.
typ.
2'-2 3/4"
3"
1 1/2"
1/2"
6"
2 1/4"
4 1/4"
3 1/2"
3"
3 1/2"
3 1/2"
3 1/2"
DRILL 5/16"Ø
HOLES THRU
DOCK - "A"
3/4" x 3 3/8" SQ.
DRILL 1/2"Ø
HOLE THRU
1/2" x 5 3/8"
2'-2 1/2"
20°
5 1/4"
3"
6"
1/2"
3"
1 1/2"
3"
4 1/4"
4 1/4"
3 1/4"
3 1/2"
4 1/4"
DRILL 11/32"Ø HOLES
THRU TOP PIECE
DOCK - "B"

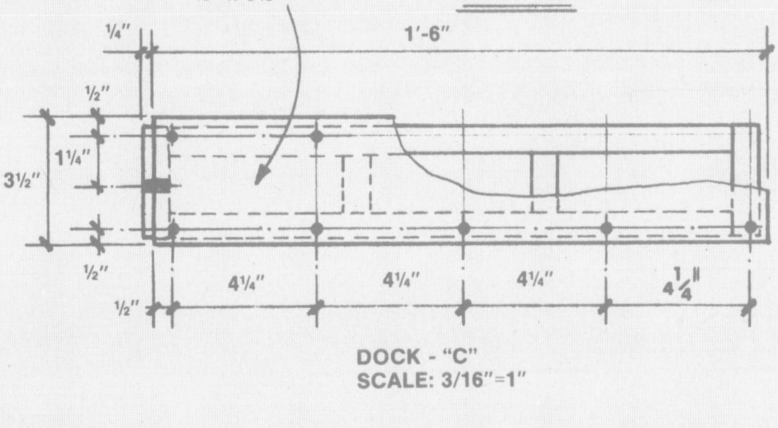

1/2" x 3 1/2"
1/4"
1'-6"
1/2"
1 1/4"
3 1/2"
1/2"
1/2"
4 1/4"
4 1/4"
4 1/4"
4 1/4"

DOCK - "C"
SCALE: 3/16"=1"

MATERIALS:

QTY.	ITEM
4'-5"	1/2" x 5 3/8" DECK
1'-6"	1/2" x 3 1/2" DECK
25'-0"	3/4" SQ. FRAME
1 ea.	3/4" x 3 3/8" SQ. BRACE
40 ea.	5/16'Ø x 1 1/8" DOWEL
40 ea.	3/16"Ø x 3/4" DOWEL
5 ea.	3/16"Ø x 2" BOLT w/ NUTS AND WASHERS

SIDEWHEELER

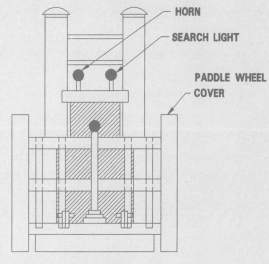

- HORN
- SEARCH LIGHT
- PADDLE WHEEL COVER

FRONT VIEW

NOTES

BOTH THE WHEEL HOUSE AND CABIN BLOCKS ARE LAMINATED FROM 5/4" STOCK. GLUE UP AND CLAMP THESE BLOCKS FIRST.

TRACE FULL SIZE PATTERNS DIRECTLY ONTO THE WOOD. BE SURE TO MARK HOLE LOCATIONS FOR DRILLING. TEMPORARILY TACK ALL DECKS TOGETHER AND DRILL COLUMN SUPPORT HOLES ALL AT THE SAME TIME.

TO FINISH, USE TWO COATS OF URETHANE GLOSS SPAR VARNISH OVER ALL AND A THIRD COAT TO HULL. SAND BEFORE AND BETWEEN COATS. USE A FAST DRYING ENAMEL PAINT FOR THE EAGLE DESIGN.

TRIM EDGES OF DECKS, WHEEL HOUSE ROOF AND SMOKE STACKS WITH AUTO PIN STRIPE TAPE IF SO DESIRED. WE RECOMMEND 3M BRAND TAPE.

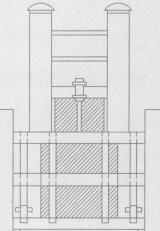

BACK VIEW

CROSS TIE BRACE
3/16" DIA DOWEL
X 1-1/2" 2 PC.

CROSS TIE 5/16"
DOWEL X 3" LG.
DRILL 2 HOLES
1/8" DEEP 2 PC.

1" PLUG BUTTON

SMOKE STACK
1" DIA. DOWEL
5-1/4" LG.

5/16" DIA. DRILL
1/4" DEEP

7/8"

1-1/2"

7/8"

13/16"

HATCHED AREA IS CABIN BLOCKS OR WHEEL HOUSE

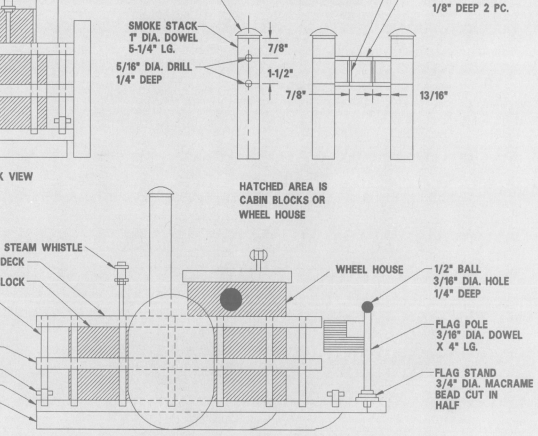

- STEAM WHISTLE
- UPPER DECK
- CABIN BLOCK
- DECK SUPPORT 5/16" DIA. DOWEL X 4" LG. 14 PCS.
- MIDDLE DECK
- DOCK TIE
- LOWER DECK
- HULL
- WHEEL HOUSE
- 1/2" BALL 3/16" DIA. HOLE 1/4" DEEP
- FLAG POLE 3/16" DIA. DOWEL X 4" LG.
- FLAG STAND 3/4" DIA. MACRAME BEAD CUT IN HALF

SIDE VIEW

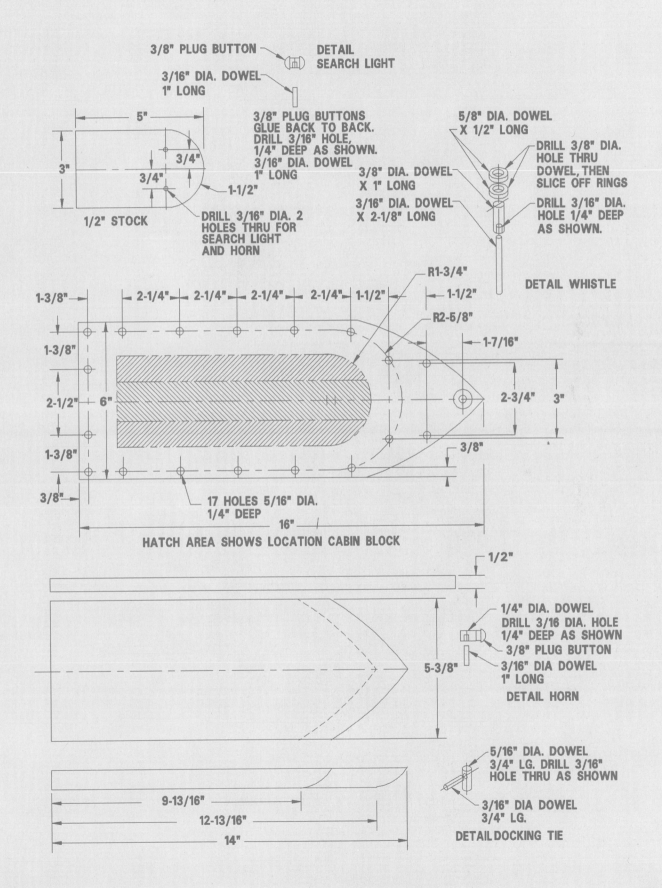

3/8" PLUG BUTTON

DETAIL SEARCH LIGHT

3/16" DIA. DOWEL 1" LONG

3/8" PLUG BUTTONS GLUE BACK TO BACK. DRILL 3/16" HOLE, 1/4" DEEP AS SHOWN. 3/16" DIA. DOWEL 1" LONG

5"

3"

3/4"

3/4"

1-1/2"

1/2" STOCK

DRILL 3/16" DIA. 2 HOLES THRU FOR SEARCH LIGHT AND HORN

5/8" DIA. DOWEL X 1/2" LONG

3/8" DIA. DOWEL X 1" LONG

3/16" DIA. DOWEL X 2-1/8" LONG

DRILL 3/8" DIA. HOLE THRU DOWEL, THEN SLICE OFF RINGS

DRILL 3/16" DIA. HOLE 1/4" DEEP AS SHOWN.

DETAIL WHISTLE

1-3/8"   2-1/4"   2-1/4"   2-1/4"   2-1/4"   1-1/2"   1-1/2"

R1-3/4"

R2-5/8"

1-7/16"

1-3/8"

2-1/2"

6"

2-3/4"   3"

1-3/8"

3/8"

3/8"

17 HOLES 5/16" DIA. 1/4" DEEP

16"

HATCH AREA SHOWS LOCATION CABIN BLOCK

1/2"

1/4" DIA. DOWEL DRILL 3/16 DIA. HOLE 1/4" DEEP AS SHOWN

3/8" PLUG BUTTON

3/16" DIA DOWEL 1" LONG

DETAIL HORN

5-3/8"

5/16" DIA. DOWEL 3/4" LG. DRILL 3/16" HOLE THRU AS SHOWN

3/16" DIA DOWEL 3/4" LG.

DETAIL DOCKING TIE

9-13/16"

12-13/16"

14"

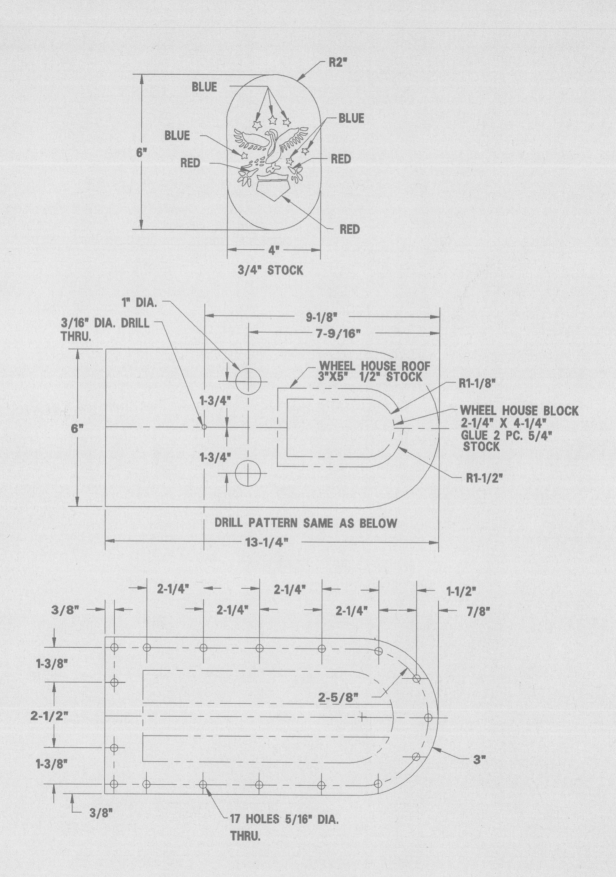

R2"

BLUE

BLUE

BLUE

RED

RED

RED

6"

4"

3/4" STOCK

1" DIA.

3/16" DIA. DRILL THRU.

9-1/8"

7-9/16"

WHEEL HOUSE ROOF 3"X5" 1/2" STOCK

R1-1/8"

WHEEL HOUSE BLOCK 2-1/4" X 4-1/4" GLUE 2 PC. 5/4" STOCK

R1-1/2"

1-3/4"

1-3/4"

6"

DRILL PATTERN SAME AS BELOW

13-1/4"

2-1/4"

2-1/4"

1-1/2"

3/8"

2-1/4"

2-1/4"

2-1/4"

7/8"

1-3/8"

2-5/8"

2-1/2"

1-3/8"

3"

3/8"

17 HOLES 5/16" DIA. THRU.

TUGBOAT

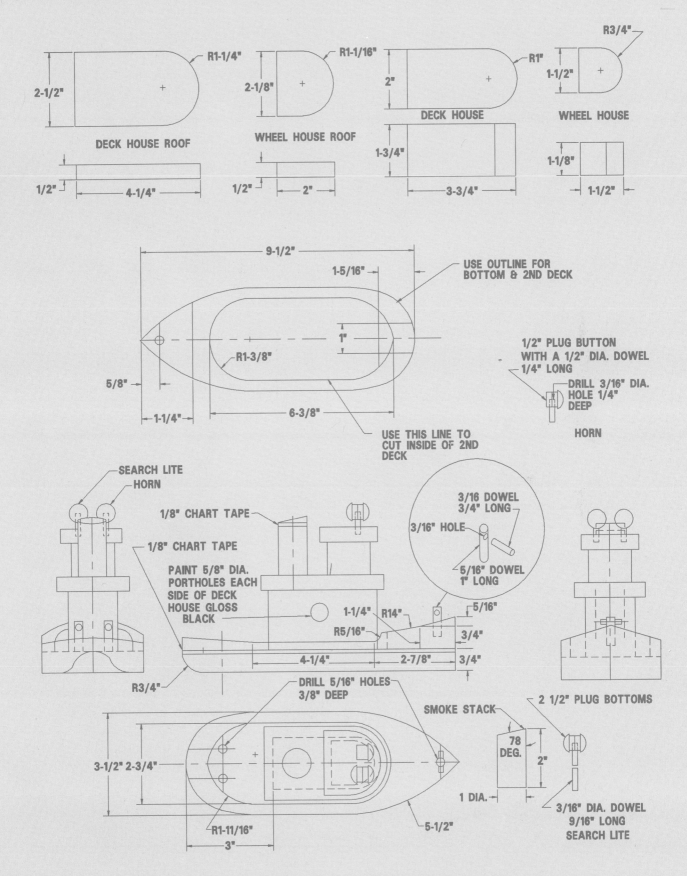

DECK HOUSE ROOF

R1-1/4"

2-1/2"

1/2"

4-1/4"

WHEEL HOUSE ROOF

R1-1/16"

2-1/8"

1/2"

2"

DECK HOUSE

R1"

2"

1-3/4"

3-3/4"

WHEEL HOUSE

R3/4"

1-1/2"

1-1/8"

1-1/2"

9-1/2"

1-5/16"

USE OUTLINE FOR
BOTTOM & 2ND DECK

1"

R1-3/8"

5/8"

1-1/4"

6-3/8"

USE THIS LINE TO
CUT INSIDE OF 2ND
DECK

1/2" PLUG BUTTON
WITH A 1/2" DIA. DOWEL
1/4" LONG

DRILL 3/16" DIA.
HOLE 1/4"
DEEP

HORN

SEARCH LITE
HORN

1/8" CHART TAPE

1/8" CHART TAPE

PAINT 5/8" DIA.
PORTHOLES EACH
SIDE OF DECK
HOUSE GLOSS
BLACK

1-1/4" R14"

R5/16"

4-1/4"   2-7/8"   3/4"

R3/4"

3/16 DOWEL
3/4" LONG

3/16" HOLE

5/16" DOWEL
1" LONG

5/16"

3/4"

DRILL 5/16" HOLES
3/8" DEEP

SMOKE STACK

3-1/2" 2-3/4"

R1-11/16"

3"

5-1/2"

78
DEG.

1 DIA.

2"

2 1/2" PLUG BOTTOMS

3/16" DIA. DOWEL
9/16" LONG
SEARCH LITE

TWO-MASTED SCHOONER

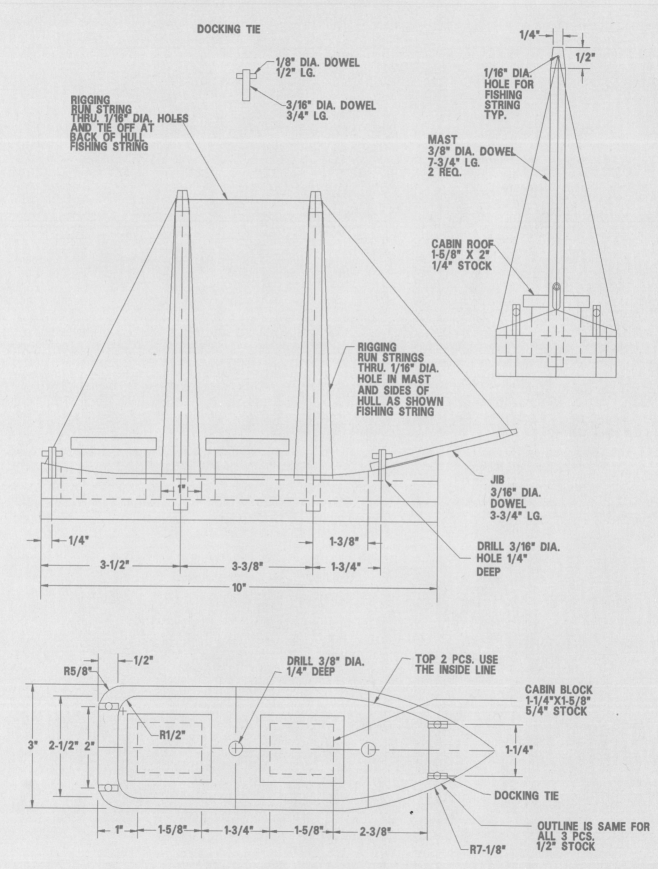

DOCKING TIE

1/8" DIA. DOWEL
1/2" LG.

3/16" DIA. DOWEL
3/4" LG.

1/4"

1/2"

1/16" DIA.
HOLE FOR
FISHING
STRING
TYP.

RIGGING
RUN STRING
THRU. 1/16" DIA. HOLES
AND TIE OFF AT
BACK OF HULL
FISHING STRING

MAST
3/8" DIA. DOWEL
7-3/4" LG.
2 REQ.

CABIN ROOF
1-5/8" X 2"
1/4" STOCK

RIGGING
RUN STRINGS
THRU. 1/16" DIA.
HOLE IN MAST
AND SIDES OF
HULL AS SHOWN
FISHING STRING

JIB
3/16" DIA.
DOWEL
3-3/4" LG.

DRILL 3/16" DIA.
HOLE 1/4"
DEEP

1"

1/4"

1-3/8"

3-1/2"

3-3/8"

1-3/4"

10"

R5/8"

1/2"

DRILL 3/8" DIA.
1/4" DEEP

TOP 2 PCS. USE
THE INSIDE LINE

CABIN BLOCK
1-1/4"X1-5/8"
5/4" STOCK

R1/2"

3"

2-1/2"

2"

1-1/4"

1"

1-5/8"

1-3/4"

1-5/8"

2-3/8"

DOCKING TIE

OUTLINE IS SAME FOR
ALL 3 PCS.
1/2" STOCK

R7-1/8"

MARINA CRANE

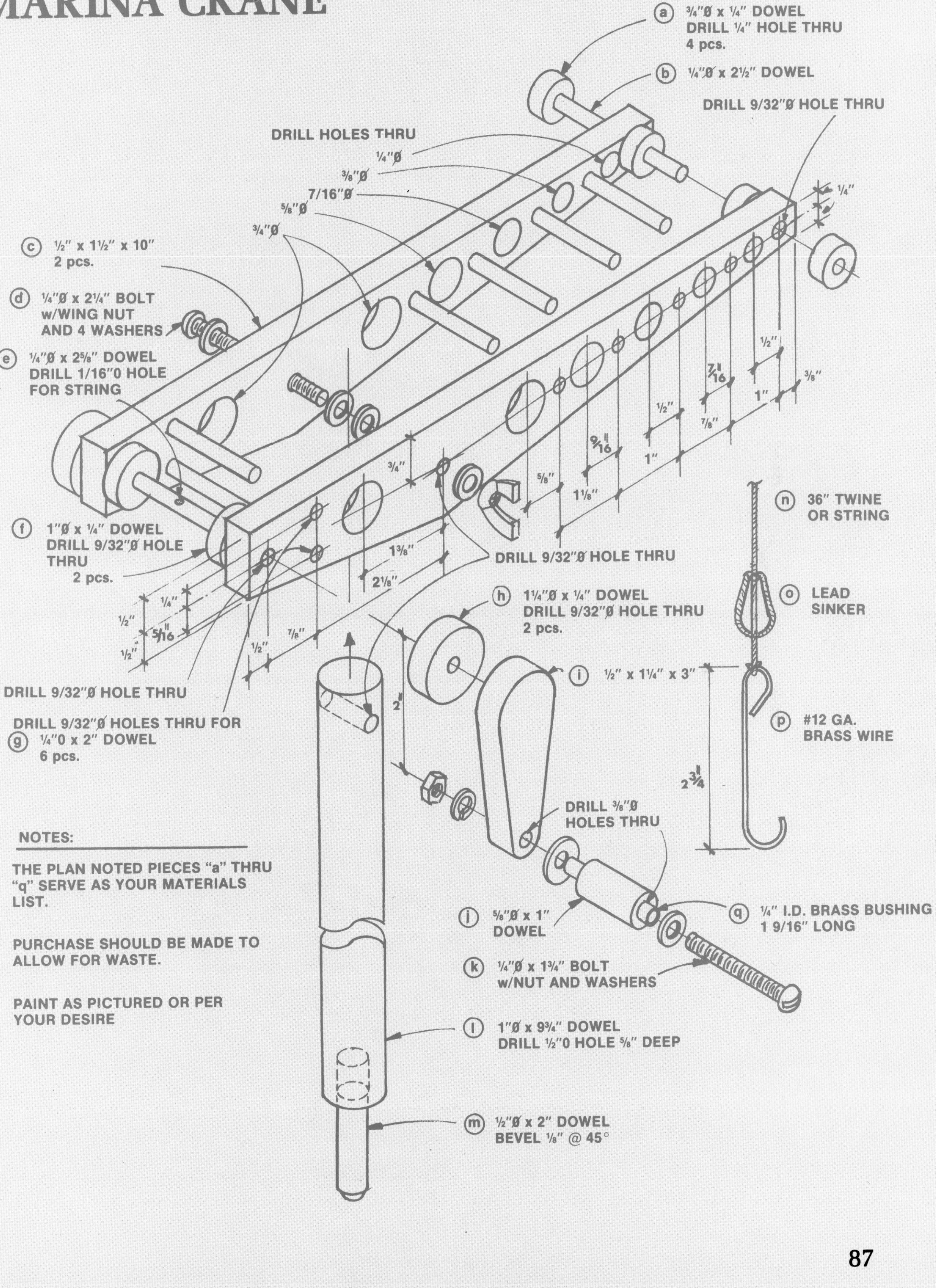

(a) ¾"Ø x ¼" DOWEL
DRILL ¼" HOLE THRU
4 pcs.
(b) ¼"Ø x 2½" DOWEL
DRILL 9/32"Ø HOLE THRU
DRILL HOLES THRU
¼"Ø
⅜"Ø
7/16"Ø
⅝"Ø
¾"Ø
¼"
(c) ½" x 1½" x 10"
2 pcs.
(d) ¼"Ø x 2¼" BOLT
w/WING NUT
AND 4 WASHERS
(e) ¼"Ø x 2⅝" DOWEL
DRILL 1/16"0 HOLE
FOR STRING
½"
⅜"
7/16
1"
½"
⅞"
9/16
1"
¾"
⅝"
1⅛"
(n) 36" TWINE
OR STRING
(f) 1"Ø x ¼" DOWEL
DRILL 9/32"Ø HOLE
THRU
2 pcs.
1⅜"
2⅛"
DRILL 9/32"Ø HOLE THRU
(o) LEAD
SINKER
(h) 1¼"Ø x ¼" DOWEL
DRILL 9/32"Ø HOLE THRU
2 pcs.
¼"
½"
5/16
½"
½"
⅞"
(i) ½" x 1¼" x 3"
DRILL 9/32"Ø HOLE THRU
2"
DRILL 9/32"Ø HOLES THRU FOR
(g) ¼"0 x 2" DOWEL
6 pcs.
(p) #12 GA.
BRASS WIRE
2¾
DRILL ⅜"Ø
HOLES THRU
(j) ⅝"Ø x 1"
DOWEL
(q) ¼" I.D. BRASS BUSHING
1 9/16" LONG
(k) ¼"Ø x 1¾" BOLT
w/NUT AND WASHERS
(l) 1"Ø x 9¾" DOWEL
DRILL ½"0 HOLE ⅝" DEEP
(m) ½"Ø x 2" DOWEL
BEVEL ⅛" @ 45°

NOTES:

THE PLAN NOTED PIECES "a" THRU "q" SERVE AS YOUR MATERIALS LIST.

PURCHASE SHOULD BE MADE TO ALLOW FOR WASTE.

PAINT AS PICTURED OR PER YOUR DESIRE

BENTWOOD DOLL BUGGY

This delightful all-lined doll buggy with its two-position wood shade hood is just the thing for your special little friend. A perfect buggy to show off a doll on a morning stroll. After the stroll, the doll can snuggle down in warmth, comfort and beauty for her afternoon nap. Wheels are turned on lathe. Bentwood is a simple system. Size: 12″ wide, 30″ high, and 30″ long, including handle.

DOLL BUGGY

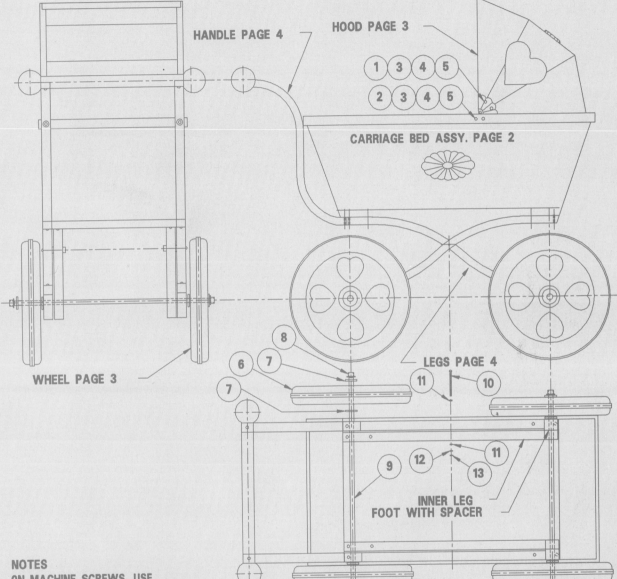

HANDLE PAGE 4

HOOD PAGE 3

CARRIAGE BED ASSY. PAGE 2

WHEEL PAGE 3

LEGS PAGE 4

INNER LEG
FOOT WITH SPACER

NOTES
ON MACHINE SCREWS, USE
WASHERS AS SHIMS BETWEEN
HINGES AND WOOD AS NECESSARY
TO HAVE MATING BRASS PLATES
MEET EVENLY AND WORK
SMOOTHLY.

STUDY THE POSITION OF THE
UNDERCARRIAGE PARTS CAREFULLY

NOTE THE SPACERS FACE OUTWARD
ON THE FEET OF THE INNER BENT
WOOD LEGS

THE SPACERS ON THE OUTER LEGS
FACE INWARD.

SEE PAGE 4 FOR DETAIL ON
BENT WOOD LEG CONSTRUCTION

NO.	PCS.	DESCRIPTION
1	8	1" #7 FLT. HD. MACH. SCREW BRASS
2	8	5/8" #7 FLT HD. MACH. SCREW BRASS
3	8	FLAT WASHER 1/8" I.D. BRASS
4	8	LOCK WASHER 1/8" I.D. BRASS
5	8	1/8" ACORN NUT BRASS
6	4	WHEEL 10" DIA. WOOD
7	8	FLAT WASHER 3/8" I.D. BRASS
8	4	3/8" DIA. PUSH NUT
9	2	AXLE 3/8" DIA. X 16" LONG STEEL
10	2	2" #7 RD. HD. MACH. SCREW BRASS
11	4	FLAT WASHER 1/8" I.D. BRASS
12	2	LOCK WASHER 1/8" I.D. BRASS
13	2	1/8" ACORN NUT

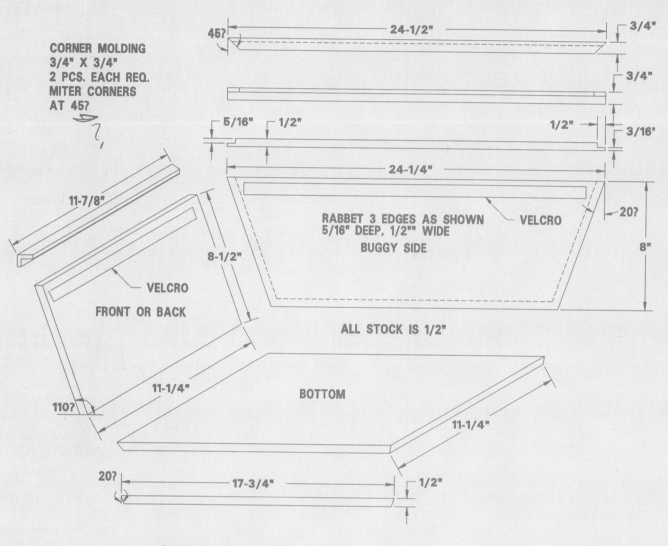

CORNER MOLDING
3/4" X 3/4"
2 PCS. EACH REQ.
MITER CORNERS
AT 45?

45? 24-1/2" 3/4"

3/4"

5/16" 1/2" 1/2" 3/16"

24-1/4"

11-7/8"

RABBET 3 EDGES AS SHOWN
5/16" DEEP, 1/2"" WIDE   VELCRO

BUGGY SIDE

20?

8"

8-1/2"

VELCRO

FRONT OR BACK

ALL STOCK IS 1/2"

11-1/4" BOTTOM

11-1/4"

110?

20? 17-3/4" 1/2"

CARRIAGE BED ASSEMBLY

NOTES

SIDES PIECES ARE RABBETED TO
ALLOW FOR MORE GLUING SURFACE
AND TO ALIGN PARTS
GLUE AND USE FINISHING NAILS. SET
NAILS AND PUTTY WHEN FINISHING.
VELCRO STRIPS ARE ADDED TO TOP
EDGES AS SHOWN TO ATTACH LINER.

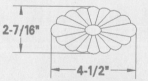

2-7/16"

4-1/2"

LARGE OVAL WOOD
APPLIQUE TO BE
PLACED IN THE
CENTER OF CARRIAGE
BED SIDE PANELS
SEE PAGE 1

1-1/2" DIA.

1-1/2" WOOD ROSETTE
PLACE IN CENTER OF
HOOD PANEL

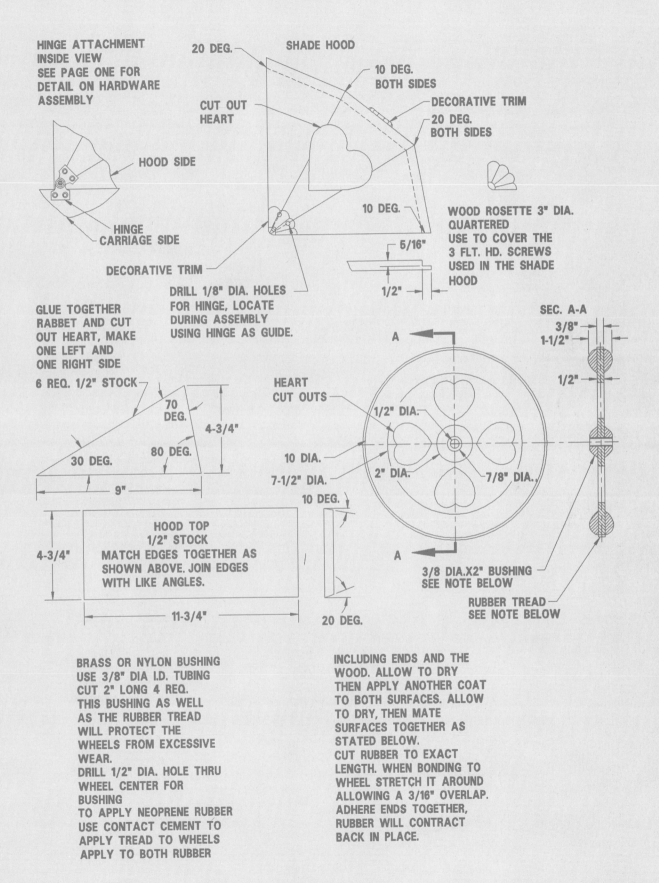

HINGE ATTACHMENT
INSIDE VIEW
SEE PAGE ONE FOR
DETAIL ON HARDWARE
ASSEMBLY

20 DEG.

SHADE HOOD

10 DEG.
BOTH SIDES

DECORATIVE TRIM

20 DEG.
BOTH SIDES

CUT OUT
HEART

HOOD SIDE

HINGE
CARRIAGE SIDE

DECORATIVE TRIM

10 DEG.

WOOD ROSETTE 3" DIA.
QUARTERED
USE TO COVER THE
3 FLT. HD. SCREWS
USED IN THE SHADE
HOOD

5/16"

1/2"

DRILL 1/8" DIA. HOLES
FOR HINGE, LOCATE
DURING ASSEMBLY
USING HINGE AS GUIDE.

GLUE TOGETHER
RABBET AND CUT
OUT HEART, MAKE
ONE LEFT AND
ONE RIGHT SIDE

6 REQ. 1/2" STOCK

70 DEG.

4-3/4"

80 DEG.

30 DEG.

9"

SEC. A-A

3/8"

1-1/2"

1/2"

HEART
CUT OUTS

1/2" DIA.

10 DIA.

7-1/2" DIA.

2" DIA.

7/8" DIA.

A

A

HOOD TOP
1/2" STOCK
MATCH EDGES TOGETHER AS
SHOWN ABOVE. JOIN EDGES
WITH LIKE ANGLES.

4-3/4"

10 DEG.

20 DEG.

11-3/4"

3/8 DIA.X2" BUSHING
SEE NOTE BELOW

RUBBER TREAD
SEE NOTE BELOW

BRASS OR NYLON BUSHING
USE 3/8" DIA I.D. TUBING
CUT 2" LONG 4 REQ.
THIS BUSHING AS WELL
AS THE RUBBER TREAD
WILL PROTECT THE
WHEELS FROM EXCESSIVE
WEAR.
DRILL 1/2" DIA. HOLE THRU
WHEEL CENTER FOR
BUSHING
TO APPLY NEOPRENE RUBBER
USE CONTACT CEMENT TO
APPLY TREAD TO WHEELS
APPLY TO BOTH RUBBER

INCLUDING ENDS AND THE
WOOD. ALLOW TO DRY
THEN APPLY ANOTHER COAT
TO BOTH SURFACES. ALLOW
TO DRY, THEN MATE
SURFACES TOGETHER AS
STATED BELOW.
CUT RUBBER TO EXACT
LENGTH. WHEN BONDING TO
WHEEL STRETCH IT AROUND
ALLOWING A 3/16" OVERLAP.
ADHERE ENDS TOGETHER,
RUBBER WILL CONTRACT
BACK IN PLACE.

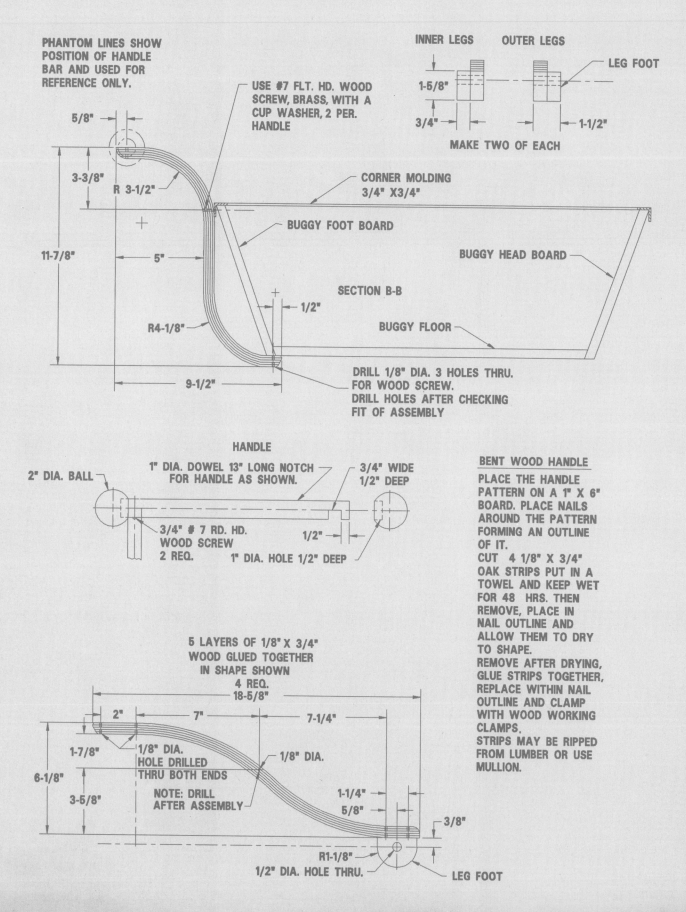

PHANTOM LINES SHOW
POSITION OF HANDLE
BAR AND USED FOR
REFERENCE ONLY.

INNER LEGS   OUTER LEGS

LEG FOOT

1-5/8"

3/4"   1-1/2"

MAKE TWO OF EACH

USE #7 FLT. HD. WOOD
SCREW, BRASS, WITH A
CUP WASHER, 2 PER.
HANDLE

5/8"

3-3/8"

R 3-1/2"

CORNER MOLDING
3/4" X3/4"

BUGGY FOOT BOARD

BUGGY HEAD BOARD

11-7/8"

5"

SECTION B-B

1/2"

R4-1/8"

BUGGY FLOOR

9-1/2"

DRILL 1/8" DIA. 3 HOLES THRU.
FOR WOOD SCREW.
DRILL HOLES AFTER CHECKING
FIT OF ASSEMBLY

HANDLE

2" DIA. BALL

1" DIA. DOWEL 13" LONG NOTCH
FOR HANDLE AS SHOWN.

3/4" WIDE
1/2" DEEP

3/4" # 7 RD. HD.
WOOD SCREW
2 REQ.

1/2"

1" DIA. HOLE 1/2" DEEP

BENT WOOD HANDLE

PLACE THE HANDLE
PATTERN ON A 1" X 6"
BOARD. PLACE NAILS
AROUND THE PATTERN
FORMING AN OUTLINE
OF IT.
CUT 4 1/8" X 3/4"
OAK STRIPS PUT IN A
TOWEL AND KEEP WET
FOR 48 HRS. THEN
REMOVE, PLACE IN
NAIL OUTLINE AND
ALLOW THEM TO DRY
TO SHAPE.
REMOVE AFTER DRYING,
GLUE STRIPS TOGETHER,
REPLACE WITHIN NAIL
OUTLINE AND CLAMP
WITH WOOD WORKING
CLAMPS.
STRIPS MAY BE RIPPED
FROM LUMBER OR USE
MULLION.

5 LAYERS OF 1/8" X 3/4"
WOOD GLUED TOGETHER
IN SHAPE SHOWN
4 REQ.

18-5/8"

2"   7"   7-1/4"

1-7/8"

1/8" DIA.
HOLE DRILLED
THRU BOTH ENDS

1/8" DIA.

6-1/8"

3-5/8"

NOTE: DRILL
AFTER ASSEMBLY

1-1/4"

5/8"

3/8"

R1-1/8"

1/2" DIA. HOLE THRU.

LEG FOOT

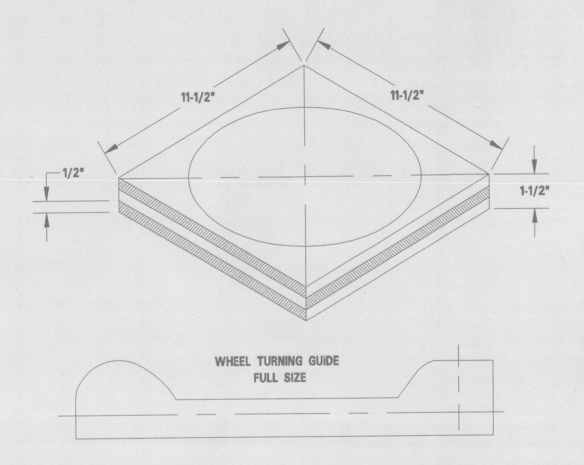

11-1/2"

11-1/2"

1/2"

1-1/2"

WHEEL TURNING GUIDE
FULL SIZE

NOTES

STUDY PLANS CAREFULLY BEFORE BEGINNING
CONSTRUCTION.

START WITH THE BENT WOOD PIECES AND
THE WHEEL BLOCKS. WHILE THESE ARE
CLAMPED AND DRYING YOU CAN PROCEED
WITH OTHER CONSTRUCTION.

SAND SURFACES WHERE NEEDED, WHERE
FINISHING NAIL ARE USED, SET NAILS, PUTTY
NAIL HOLES WHEN FINISHING.

TO FINISH USE STAIN OF CHOICE, THEN TWO
2 COATS OF SEALER FIRST THEN 1 COAT OF
POLYURETHANE GLOSS VARNISH, SANDING
BETWEEN COATS.

WHEEL BLOCK

GLUE TOGETHER 3 PCS. OF 1/2" X12"
LUMBER AS SHOWN, CROSS LAPPING
THE GRAIN. THIS WILL HELP PREVENT
WARPING.

ROUGH CUT WHEEL OVERSIZE, DRILL
1/16" DIA. PILOT HOLE THRU CENTER
TO AID IN DRILLING BUSHING HOLE
LATER.

TURN WHEEL ON A LATHE USING THE
GUIDE.

BE SURE THE CENTER HOLE IS
DRILLED STRAIGHT TO INSURE PROPER
ROTATION.

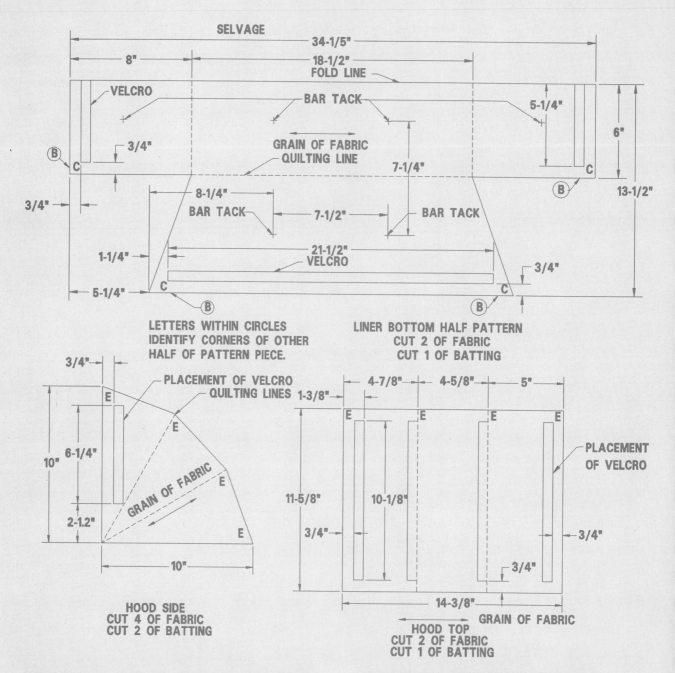

SELVAGE

34-1/5"

8"

18-1/2"
FOLD LINE

VELCRO

BAR TACK

5-1/4"

3/4"

GRAIN OF FABRIC
QUILTING LINE

7-1/4"

6"

B
C

B
C

13-1/2"

3/4"

8-1/4"

BAR TACK

7-1/2"

BAR TACK

1-1/4"

21-1/2"
VELCRO

3/4"

5-1/4"

C

C

B

B

LETTERS WITHIN CIRCLES
IDENTIFY CORNERS OF OTHER
HALF OF PATTERN PIECE.

LINER BOTTOM HALF PATTERN
CUT 2 OF FABRIC
CUT 1 OF BATTING

3/4"

PLACEMENT OF VELCRO
QUILTING LINES

E

E

10"

6-1/4"

GRAIN OF FABRIC

E

2-1.2"

E

10"

HOOD SIDE
CUT 4 OF FABRIC
CUT 2 OF BATTING

4-7/8"

4-5/8"

5"

1-3/8"

E

E

E

E

11-5/8"

10-1/8"

PLACEMENT
OF VELCRO

3/4"

3/4"

3/4"

14-3/8"

GRAIN OF FABRIC

HOOD TOP
CUT 2 OF FABRIC
CUT 1 OF BATTING

WITH RIGHT SIDES OF TOP TOGETHER, SEW AROUND EDGE OF PIECE USING 1/2" SEAM ALLOWANCE, LEAVING 3" OPENING FOR TURNING. TURN RIGHT SIDE OUT, HAND STITCH OPENING, AND PRESS.

PIN ALONG QUILTING LINE AND STITCH THROUGH ALL THICKNESSES.

SEW THE SIDE PIECES OF HOOD LINING IN A SIMILAR MANNER. WITH RIGHT SIDES TOGETHER, SEW AROUND EDGES, LEAVING 3" OPENING. TURN RIGHT SIDE OUT, HAND STITCH OPENING AND PRESS. REPEAT FOR OTHER SIDE.

PIN AND STITCH ALONG QUILTING LINES.

MATCHING QUILTING LINES AND E POINTS OF SIDE AND TOP, CURVE TOP PIECE AND PIN TO SIDE, BUTTING FINISHED SEAMS TOGETHER. VELCRO SHOULD BE ON THE SAME SIDE ON EACH PIECE. ZIG-ZAG OR HAND SEW ALONG THIS SEAM, CATCHING BOTH EDGES AND SEWING TOGETHER. REPEAT FOR OTHER SIDE OF HOOD LINING.

SEW LACE ALL AROUND OUTER EDGE OF LINING. SEW LACE CLOSE TO EDGE AND ON THE SAME SIDE VELCRO IS ON. HAND STITCH CUT ENDS OF LACE TOGETHER.

Index & Price List
for Regular-sized Plans

Please include the following shipping and handling on all orders (all prices in U.S. dollars):

United States—lower 48	$3.75
Alaska, Hawaii, Canada	$7.00
All Other Countries	$14.00

Wisconsin residents add 5%

MC and VISA accepted with account number and expiration date.

Send plan orders to:

Timeless Designs, Inc.
545 E. Milwaukee Street
Whitewater, WI 53190

Toll Free for orders	(800) 765-0176
Fax	(414) 473-6112